Enriching Faith Through
Family Celebrations

Sandra DeGidio

Enriching Faith
through
Family Celebrations

XXIII

TWENTY-THIRD PUBLICATIONS
Mystic, Connecticut

Art by Jeanne Bright

Twenty-Third Publications
185 Willow Street
P.O. Box 180
Mystic, CT 06355
(203) 536-2611

ISBN 0-89622-381-7
Library of Congress Catalog Card Number 88-51303

CONTENTS

Enriching Faith Through Family Celebrations

INTRODUCTION

Children learn the basic human and Christian values better within the family circle than in the best of schools. Family ritual is the most effective method in the religious formation of families because ritual is a family's and a community's fullest expression of itself. There are few, if any, family rituals that fail to share faith.

That, in a nutshell, was the premise of my earlier book for parish staff personnel, *Sharing Faith in the Family*. At that time I had been involved in family ministry and catechesis for nearly ten years. My experience with families had convinced me that ritual was the best method of family and Christian faith-growth and development better than the best of schools or the best religious education programs, methods, or texts. One of the most repeated requests from parents then was "Give us some ideas our family can observe and celebrate the liturgical seasons together." The need today is the same. So is my conviction that the family is the best transmitter of religious formation, faith, and values, and that the best way that a family can transmit or share that faith and those values is through ritual.

Once, a woman approached me after a talk I had given, carrying a tattered copy of my 1980 book, to tell me how valuable the family rituals had been for her family and for numerous military families around the world with whom she had shared the book and the rituals. Moreover, families I had worked with for eight years in a large suburban Minneapolis parish still keep in touch with me and I have watched their children continue to grow in faith with the help of the rituals included here, which have been part of their lives.

Those families have used and developed for themselves many of the rituals described in this little volume. In some cases, I have experienced these rituals with them and have seen them to be successful. I have also observed the results of family faith that has developed from the celebration of these rituals.

I have had the honor of serving as confirmation sponsor for some of the children of those families and been able to witness the depth of faith that family ritualizing produced in those children. I have also suffered with some of those parents who patiently helped their children through a searching stage of faith—while those children, for a time, rejected the faith that their parents had shared with them. And I have watched while some of those same children have grown into marriage and parenthood, and now pass on to their families the family rituals and traditions that they experienced as children.

This book is for all of you who were "ankle biters" way back when I first worked with you and your parents eighteen years ago. It is for you, and it is for your children.

Yes, I still believe, because of what I have seen and heard, that the family's ritualizing of its faith is the best means of family faith sharing, growth, and development. For all of you who share my belief, or who think the idea might have some credence, I offer this little book as gift. May it become totally gift as it is shared by each of you. In that sharing, may you reveal your own precious giftedness to one another and bring to each other the promise and reality of Christian faith.

PART I

THE MEANING
OF RITUALS

CHAPTER
— 1 —

RITUAL MAKING IN FAMILIES

When my sister was married, the reception was one of those marvelous Italian extravaganzas. Somewhere between the fourth course and dessert, my father stood up to call for a toast. The clinking of knives on glasses silenced the 200 guests. Dad stood, wine glass raised high, pausing just long enough and then in his strong baritone voice sang:

> Good-bye, little darling, we're parting,
> Parting don't always mean good-bye.
> You found someone new,
> And he'll be good to you
> Good-bye, little darling, good-bye.
> Good-bye, little darling, I'll miss you
> Just like the stars will miss the sky.
> Though we'll be apart
> You'll always have my heart
> Good-bye, little darling, good-bye.

Finishing his song two verses before he really wanted to because my sister was crying and the groom was visibly nervous, my father drained his wine glass and watched as his guests did the same. Then he went over and kissed the bride, shook hands with and hugged the groom while he whispered something in his ear. Then he called for the cutting of the wedding cake.

As I reflect on this incident, I realize that my father had just created and led us all through a perfectly structured ritual. He had never studied ritual, but ritual had always been a part of his own family life. Consequently, it had been an important part of our family life. It came natural to him.

That's the way ritual making is cultivated in each of us— we learn it by participating in it. To move from being participant to being creator or presider at a ritual requires what my father exemplified at my sister's wedding: a sense of timing and of dramatic action, an awareness of the story being celebrated, and a willingness to express the feeling and faith of the moment with those present.

In his book, *Feast of Fools*, Harvey Cox points out that human beings are by their very nature creatures who not only work and think but who sing, dance, pray, tell stories, and celebrate. He calls us *homo festivus*. He maintains that no other creature we know of relives the legends of his forebears, blows out candles on a birthday cake, or dresses up and pretends to be someone else. Human beings, he says, "are natural ritualizers."

Because ritual is an integral part of life, it is at the center of the church's life. We seem to forget this or, at best, do not give enough credit to the prominence that ritual plays in our lives and to the need we all have for it.

In the past we used to call these rituals "family devotions." As time went on, we became aware that our rituals had become merely prescribed or mechanical procedures, formal structures without heart to be followed for religious obligation. They no longer flowed from our sense of family, our common experiences, our needs, our imagination, or our sense of immediacy with our history.

Today families are at the point of developing a new level of appreciation and incorporation of ritual into their lives. This does not mean a return to rituals that became meaningless because of cultural changes, but rather the creative development of new rituals for a new age to express the lived experiences of today, rituals that help us reflect on both our sacred and our secular experiences and see them as one.

We need new rituals that will not only carry us through crises but also through the repetitious and mundane. We need rituals that will intuitively and effectively communicate meaning to our spirits by means of story, symbol, and action. Such rituals will enhance the meaning of special moments in our lives and enable us to communicate our faith.

Ritual (the combination of myth, symbol, and action) is the most effective method to use in the religious formation and development of faith in families because it is how a family or a community expresses itself most fully. Ritual speaks to the whole person and imparts a holistic knowledge. (Western culture equates knowledge with the head. Eastern culture, including the culture from which our Scriptures come, has a much broader, more effective, and relational understanding of "knowing." Western understanding of knowledge results in science; Eastern understanding of knowledge results in poetry.)

Words, classes, books, and pictures alone—the media that characterize our common catechetical approaches—cannot adequately communicate what is in the heart. With its elements of story, symbol, and action, ritual characterizes a catechesis that reaches us and transforms us holistically.

We are natural ritualizers. Our most commonplace experiences are ritualistic: parties, parades, watching football, conventions, walking the dog, homecomings. Yet we seldom reflect on these as rituals that carry with them deeper meanings about our lives.

Children, especially, live by rituals. Watch children at play. Note the order, the predictability of the soccer game, the hopscotch, the rope jumping, the tag game. The ritual of children jumping rope is neither a mere repetitive diversion nor a conceptualized mode of instilling the values of patience, endurance, sharing, and cooperation into the child. Yet, through the repetitive ritual experience of word, symbol, and action—"blue bells, cockle shells, eensy, eeny over"—these values are made present and effective even though they are not perceived conceptually.

Ritual accomplishes two things not conveyed better through any other method of catechesis: It conveys truth concretely rather than abstractly, and it actualizes, or *real*-izes, that truth *now*. To jump rope, there are rules not to be broken, and the truth here is that without patience, endurance, sharing, and cooperation, the play is false or unreal.

In the realm of religious growth, we must recognize that there is no such thing as abstractions of faith. As abstractions, God, love, community, hope are quite unimportant. They are important only if they are actual. Their reality can be expressed best through symbols and creative play.

And ritual, in a very real sense, is creative play. Transactional analysts tell us that for religious experience and prayer to be internalized, the "adult" has to get the "parent" off the "child's" back. Ritual can help that to happen.

Through ritual we are able to express the faith which is often difficult for us to verbalize. Through ritual we enact what is in the heart.

I strongly believe that nothing accomplishes family faith-sharing as effectively as ritual, which enables the family and community to express the faith within. Children can see it concretely and can appreciate both the faith expressed and the people revealing it; they can grow from it and share their own faith concretely. Thus children become not just learners who have to know certain things in order to be Christian (as our religious education programs can often suggest), but sharers in the life and actions of the Christian community.

Parents, too, do not "teach" their children through ritual, as we narrowly use the word, but by growing in the faith themselves and expressing it, they are communicating faith to their children.

In ritual the family's story and action emerge and become one. We remember and act in symbolic ways, which bring our tradition and lives together. A celebration of the Passover Meal celebrated by the Hebrews, for example, is neither a reminiscence of a fable about some angelic boogey man who slaughtered the bad guys and saved the good guys, nor an ab-

stract formula explaining the essence of God and God's cos-
mic plan. Rather, it is a re-enactment of God's faithful love
made present here and now for all those celebrating and indeed in communion with all those who have preceded us in
the Judeo-Christian tradition. The ritual of eucharist, first
celebrated by Jesus and then by his followers as they remembered Jesus' works and actions down through the ages, expresses our present-day belief in that faithful love continu-
ing, which we ourselves now experience. The story (the
history) is ongoing in the symbol and action.

If our children are to know our faith and share in it, they
must ritualize with us, for through ritual the truths of our
faith are re-actualized and *real*-ized today. Ritual embraces
the whole content of our faith because each participant is
present as a believing person.

The goal of ritual is not to educate *per se*. No one comes to
ritual intent on learning, nor do they go away from ritual
enumerating what they have learned; but learning in fact
takes place. It is a learning that happens as a result of a past
experience reflected upon and integrated now into life, not a
learning that is a compilation of facts or memorized answers.

CHAPTER

— 2 —

ELEMENTS OF RITUAL

Myth

Myth or story in ritual conveys a truth concretely. The details of the story need not be true, but the message or reality it conveys is true. For example, the specifics of the story of George Washington's cutting down the cherry tree is probably not true, but the truth conveyed through that story is that honesty is an important virtue in the lives of Americans as modeled by our first president. Many of our stories in Scripture must be understood similarly.

In our family rituals we are presenting *the* story of God's relationship to a covenant community, a family community, and to an individual's own journey in faith. This is the message we want to convey. Too often we are so caught up in the historical, formal, or literary interpretations of Scripture that we fail to tell the story.

Using a non-religious story or a story by a contemporary author that expresses the same truth as a Scripture passage is also effective. Children's literature has many such stories. These stories are particularly palatable to children; they listen more carefully and can make the association between the story, the Scripture message, and real life with greater psychological ease. In addition, parents find that children's stories foster their own growth, since a large percentage of children's stories are in reality stories for adults because of the depth of meaning within them. To verify this, you might obtain from a library a list of award-winning children's books and spend leisure time enjoying them.

Storytelling is much more effective than story reading, whether the story be your own or someone else's. Telling the story requires that something of yourself is put into it. We cannot narrate a story without revealing something about ourselves, and when we risk telling something about ourselves, others take courage to risk similarly. We may be telling a story from Scripture, but through the telling we are also communicating a story about ourselves, our family, our community, our traditions. It is inevitable. At the same time, one cannot tell a story without sharing faith.

Facial expression (which conveys a significant part of what we are trying to communicate), inflections of the voice, eye contact, body language—all communicate more of what is within us that is meaningful to us than the mere words of the story.

Parents today are concerned that their children know Bible stories. They want to know which of the many children's Bibles on the market is the best. There are several that are good, but I recommend that parents *tell* Bible stories to their children. You will communicate your faith more effectively that way than by a children's Bible that will soon be outgrown. Moreover, your children will be more appreciative of the time spent with them and of your closeness to them during the storytelling.

One cannot tell children a story without sitting close to them. Whenever a story is told, there is a natural inclination to get as close as possible to the storyteller. Even adults lean closer when a story begins.

Film, theater, and TV can be good storytellers, too. Viewing a movie, play, or television program together as a family and then sharing its meaning is an especially effective way to share faith in the family. For example, the classic Christmas films, "Miracle on 34th Street," "It's a Wonderful Life," "The Little Match Girl," can be great opportunities for faith sharing during the Advent season. Such films as "Mask," "Chariots of Fire," "Mission," "Children of a Lesser God" can provide families with much discussion and the sharing of ideas, attitudes, and values. The same is true of stage plays such as "Fiddler on the Roof," "Man of La Mancha," "Foxfire," and many others that may come to your area.

National and local news stories can help a family become more aware of the need so many have of our prayer and action. In the winter of 1982 an Air Florida jet crashed into the Potomac River. Newspapers and news broadcasts carried the story of one passenger who kept passing on the life preserver to someone else each time it was thrown to him. Finally, when there was no one else, the rescuers prepared to bring him in, but the man had disappeared beneath the water. One family was so touched by this man's life-giving action that every evening for a week they ritualized their experience by lighting a candle and praying for the "man in the water."

Another family, so moved by the news of the homeless and hungry in their area, spent Christmas Eve working at a soup kitchen. One of their sons even gave his expensive running shoes to a man whose canvas shoes were torn and wet. The young man stood on serving trays on the cold floor for the rest of the day, and the family still enjoys retelling the story of carrying him from the kitchen to the car over snowdrifts and winter slush.

There are a number of regular weekly TV programs that if viewed and then discussed as a family can be special moments of religious formation. A program that seems to promote questionable morals, for example, can, with discussion, be a lesson in family and Christian ethics. A program with strong moral principles can serve to affirm a family's own principles. One TV program that strikes me as especially valuable to families is the Thanksgiving episode on the Bill Cosby Show in which the family tradition of carving the turkey is passed on to Theo. Similarly, episodes of other prime time TV programs can provide appropriate opportunities for families to talk about their beliefs and values.

Poetry as a message maker also has numerous possibilities. We tend to shy away from it because we fear that people will not understand it. Or if we use poetry, we are tempted to interpret it. But like Scripture or any art, when used as a message carrier, poetry must be allowed to be interpreted by the listener for the listener, or it ceases to be myth and becomes instead the vehicle for the study of that particular art piece or an occasion for a didactic sermon.

Songs, too, both religious and secular, can be storytellers. The ballads of old and of today are written precisely to do that. Rather than complain about your children's music preference, have them share its meaning for them with you, and grow together in the dialogue.

And don't forget your own family myths—stories of your ancestors, your family's heroes and heroines—which help give your family a sense of heritage and meaning. (Ancestors and their story suggest your family's charism, the gift of self.) For example, were your ancestors risk takers? Were they people who effected change? How? What is the legacy they have left you? What have each of the adults and children in your immediate family inherited from your forebears?

Here is an absolute when telling a myth or story: Never, never explain the meaning of the myth. A good myth does not need explanation; it speaks for itself because it speaks to individuals where they are. What makes myth (and ritual) so powerful for individuals is that they provide a format that captures the imagination and stirs the desire in individuals to search out the meaning within the story as it relates to their own experience and challenges them to seek new and deeper ways of living their response to the truth conveyed.

Explaining a myth is like a poet explaining the meaning of his or her poem before reciting it. The danger is that you explain what the myth means to you, not what it may mean to others. Each of us responds to myth according to our own self-awareness and our readiness to be converted. Explanation does violence to the myth and to the listeners; it is like answering questions before they are asked. Furthermore, it turns a ritual experience into a classroom experience; there is the expectation that something very specific must be learned from the story. Such action destroys the purpose of both myth making and ritual making.

This is not to say that participants cannot be asked to share what the myth says to them about their own lives. Indeed, such sharing is to be encouraged. The underlying rule is that no one's application of the myth to his or her life is to be disputed; no one's understanding of the myth is to be applied to another person. The language style of faith-sharing and ritual is characterized by abundant use of first-person singular pronouns. "I hear...," "I think...," "I feel...."

Providing this opportunity for sharing in your family helps family members appreciate one another. The experience is affirming both for parents and children. Many parents are amazed at their children's depth of faith and understanding. And, of course, children have insight into their parents' faith, and can learn that faith involves doubt, questioning, and weakness, as well as generosity, strength, and perseverance.

Some family members may get nothing out of the myth, and that is all right, too. It is important to give people the freedom to be sometimes totally untouched by the myth.

Symbol
Symbol is the second important element of ritual. Myths are powerful symbols that take place in the imagination. Other symbols incorporated into the ritual are sensuously operative, i.e., they can be touched, smelled, felt, held, tasted, seen, listened to, played with. We know the importance of utilizing the senses in the traditional education process; yet somehow in our worship and praying we have not effectively utilized even our existing ecclesial symbols, much less the natural cultural symbols that can speak just as loudly of our relationship to God.

Our lives are filled with sensuous objects capable of becoming symbols of the meaning we find in our experiences and existence. Christmas is not Christmas without Christmas trees; Easter needs decorated eggs; birthdays need cakes; autumn in most sections of the country needs multicolored leaves; Halloween gives us the opportunity to dress up and pretend to be one of our heroes or heroines for a while.

Symbols become for us what they signify; that's how power-ful they are. Did you ever try to celebrate Thanksgiving without turkey? If your children have experienced Thanksgiving with a turkey, it is nearly impossible for them to imagine the day with-out the bird.

If you ask a child about a photo, the response will reveal that for the child the photo is indeed the presence of that person: "That's my Uncle Sam." Grandparents do the same with pho-tos of grandchildren. The paper with an image on it is seldom "a picture of my grandchild"; rather, "This *is* my grandchild."

And it is not only children and grandparents for whom symbols are what they say they are. In our family, we have the custom of having a stewed-onion dish on Christmas Eve. For me, Christmas Eve always included crying while I peeled what seemed like hundreds of onions, then smelling them cook all day, and finally having to eat some. I never liked them, and my mother knew that; but everyone had to have some every year. Recently I arrived home on Christmas Eve afternoon, walked into the house, sniffed, and noticed the ab-sence of stewing onions. I barely said hello before I asked, "Where are the onions?" My mother looked at me in a hurt sort of way and said, "I know you don't like them, so I didn't make any this year."

"But Mom," I said, "it's not Christmas Eve without on-ions." So we rolled up our sleeves and began peeling onions, crying, and stewing them.

For others in my family, different Christmas Eve sym-bols signify the day: square noodles, the fried codfish that has been dried and salted and then soaked all week, or the fried bread with raisins. For my father, it was delivering presents to my parents' many godchildren. For anyone not in our family circle, each of these symbols could have an entirely different meaning. I learned in working with Na-tive Americans in northern Wisconsin, for example, that fried bread has nothing to do with Christmas for them; but I was told that if I placed under my pillow a piece of it tak-en from a wedding celebration, I would dream of a hand-some young man and be married within a year. I didn't try it, so I don't know if the symbol is indeed that powerful.

Symbols function on two levels of meaning. A symbol has an objective, conventional, or natural meaning, so that for those not of the Ojibway Indian culture or the Neopolitan ancestry, fried bread may be simply fried bread. A symbol also has a subjective or affective meaning in which there is the possibility for several different emotions or conditions that enable the symbol to signify more than it communicates on the objective level.

Symbols must function on the two levels of meaning to have their full impact. These two levels open boundless possibilities for the use of symbols. Using the natural symbols of everyday life—leaves, apples, flowers, rocks, butterflies, eggs, the sun, the moon, salt, wood—in creative ways not only helps people relate to the commonplace in their lives, but also aids in the wedding of the sacred and the secular.

The joining of sacred and secular in our lives is much needed today. People are desperately searching for spiritual renewal in Bible study, prayer groups, and any number of specially designed programs of spiritual growth and are overlooking the natural and common experiences and symbols that reveal the holiness of life. In our search we step on the violet instead of lying on the ground to hear what it might be able to tell us.

Besides the two levels of meaning, symbols perform two functions in ritual: They invite us to take meaning from them and they call us to take a stand. The second function follows from the first. Once we have discovered a meaning for ourselves in the symbol and have come face to face with the depth of our experiences, we are compelled to take a stand with regard to the meaning. Investing the symbol with meaning for ourselves and assuming a stance is inevitably followed by action based on that incorporation of the symbol into ourselves.

Perhaps one reason we fill our processes of education with so much verbiage is our desire to control what's happening. We feel safe when we can control and predict what will happen and what will supposedly be understood. To shift the emphasis from words to symbols becomes risky. Someone might miss what we think they should grasp, someone might have a different interpretation than what we anticipated. But that is the joy and power of symbol and ritual. They are creative. We throw possibilities out to people, and some of them may catch them and some may not. That's the nature of family faith sharing based on the gospel. It invites the free response: "Let the one who has ears to hear, hear; the one who has eyes to see, see."

For those who do, the meanings they catch will make a difference in their lives. They will begin to see the world and their relationships in the world in a new light. The circus will begin to have as much religious significance as the Advent wreath. The naming of the new baby will be as holy a responsibility as the child's baptism. The teachable moment will be recognized and used because they will discover the value of the ordinary and concrete in the life of faith.

Effective rituals tend to become traditional. Dolores Curran says, "*Once* is a tradition for children." She is correct, and it is also true of adults when ritual is particularly meaningful. Good ritual with its use of symbol lingers in the memory; and in lingering, it allows us to revel in its meaning long after it is over.

Symbol, like myth, is self-explanatory. Symbol, like myth, is not to be explained; let it speak for itself. Let it be missed by some. Let it be interpreted in various ways and let people share what it means to them personally. Don't worry about those who might miss the significance of the symbol. In allowing the freedom to find meaning or not find meaning, there is growth. We plant the seeds; the harvesting may occur at another time.

Ritual Action
Paul wrote, "Our bodies are temples of the Holy Spirit." It is through the body that we enact what is in our hearts. In ritual, if the myth has conveyed a concrete truth and we experience symbolic meaning that calls us to take a stand, the natural result is ritualization, acting out the deepened meaning, the renewed faith, the surprise or wonder of the moment.

For most of us North Americans, a free or large physical response is difficult, perhaps because we have been told so often that even though our bodies are temples of the Spirit, the best room in the temple is from the neck up and that's really where the Spirit dwells. The rest of the body we are not so positive about. We treat the neck down as empty rooms we rarely enter and seldom use in moments of ritual worship.

Gesture has always been part of ritual, at least in the way the celebrant held his arms and hands and genuflected. Those are not the ritual actions I refer to here. Ritual action is more. It is also the spontaneous action that comes from being called to take a stand. Both the structured gesture and the spontaneous action can happen within a particular ritual.

Although ritual is not fundamentally spontaneous, time and space should always allow for the surprising to take place. With children, surprises will happen, and ritual, in a sense, inserts a new dimension into our present situation. If the ritual does, in fact, speak to the hearts of the ritualizers, then wonder, awe, and surprise will be expressed, sometimes verbally, sometimes in a physical response. In this case, you will know that the ritual is working. You will feel it.

Ritual action also adds a celebrative note to ritual. It may be as simple as exchanging apples with one another or as complex as a dance or mime. But it is necessary because rituals must celebrate an experience. Rituals that are not celebrations are like the "old maids" at the bottom of the popcorn popper—they sizzle but they don't pop.

In short, rituals cannot be called rituals without ritual action. And the ritual action we employ can be anything that helps us *enact what is in the heart*. During a ritual action, whether it is simple or complex, not a word is spoken by the leader. Some words may be in order before or after the action, but not during it. The action speaks for itself.

The elements of ritual (myth, symbol, and action) comprise a natural structural pattern or movement. The transition from one element to another is not totally distinct as individual steps. Rather, they flow into each other and one becomes an extension of the other and enhances it.

Ritual is more a sensuous and affective experience than it is a rational one. It is difficult to define or to describe. Ritual must be *experienced*; it must be celebrated. While it cannot be easily defined or described, we almost always know it when we encounter it. When it is celebrated, there is interaction between two or more persons who consciously attempt to look toward the transcendent in the hope that the divine will be manifest anew in the present circumstances of life.

Ritual is celebrated *in the faith* that the Spirit will become present to us. This is the faith that families share in ritual. If and when the divine presence is experienced, that, too, is shared and celebrated. The mundane is broken through, and we are changed.

Mood is important to the effectiveness of the ritual; it provides a quality of buoyancy to the essential elements. In ritualizing with the family, one of the first steps is to establish the mood, to ready people to enter into the ritual. This is established in part by tending to the environment where the ritual will take place. How can you best use the setting where the ritual will take place? What will be the background for the ritual: what objects, what activity, what positioning of chairs, tables, symbols, sounds, or music?

This setting of mood can also be done with some simple, but brief dialoge with the family. People will come to ritual from various pleasant or unpleasant situations. There may have been a family argument around the dinner table, a quiet study time, a hard day at work, or an exhuberant play time in the family. The mood-setting aspect of the ritual structure must help the family move from the past moods or events to the present, if they are going to enter the ritual fully and if it is to have its full impact upon them.

The mood continues to be developed by the story or myth that is told. The story, which may be as simple as an explanation of the why and how of the ritual, helps the family to move from where they are now to where they may be led, given their openness to the revelation of the story.

Good ritual, like good drama, draws people into itself; and families, especially children, will be responsive. The Spirit is moving. Therefore, another aspect of ritual is its potential for surprise. The ritual may be carefully planned and structured on paper or in someone's mind; but all must remain flexible to what is said, to what happens. They must listen and be attentive and ready to change pace, follow the mood, expand the symbolism or story, and act responsively. Rituals are created in part while they are being enacted. Immediacy is the heart of ritual, which explains why it is such a powerful medium for effective faith sharing. Ritual is faith happening here and now.

Ritual might be described as "wasting time with the Lord." A good ritual envelops us so that we forget what mood or situation we came from, rise above it, and are changed. Even if some family members (often teens) approach ritual with a "let's-get-it-over" attitude, a good ritual will lift them above themselves into that sense of timelessness or immediacy. Of course, those family members may not admit that.

CHAPTER

— 3 —

BY THEIR RITES YOU
SHALL KNOW THEM

Although I have just described the elements of ritual, which, in the final analysis, is an art that each family must cultivate. Ritual making is everyone's art.

Family occasions can be very simply, yet significantly, celebrated at home: birth, the naming of a baby, spring cleaning, yard raking, the first date, endings, beginnings, death as well as birthdays, anniversaries, and liturgical seasons. Doing this helps parents and families recognize teachable moments on which they can capitalize.

Family ritual need not be couched in traditional praying. The one thing that ritual ought to help us discover is prayer in the ordinary; God can be encountered while playing in leaves, doing laundry, or appreciating a mountain, a work of art, a jack pine. We learn to find Christ the Clown at the circus or in a parade, and most of all, to recognize the Christ in ourselves and in our neighbors.

Once parents have created a few rituals and children have

participated in them, they will want to take over the ritual making. Once your family begins experiencing success with home rituals, the rituals can be shared with other families. The encouragement one family offers will be affirmation for others and excite them about their own giftedness.

Using ritual in the family can help capitalize on what are customary secular rituals and help them enjoy a sense of holiness, of sacredness in the seemingly profane. To quote Gerard Pottebaum, who says in his marvelous little book, *The Rites of People*:

> People come in touch with the sacred by discovering the holiness of the profane. We express this discovery—we make holiness tangible—through the dramatic art of ritual making. In this creative action we come to enjoy a new spirit. We come to realize an even greater discovery, the joy of our lives: that we ourselves are the tangible expression of a Holy Spirit. That is something to parade through town about.

Halloween is an example of how this can be done. Generally, we have come to view Halloween as a "purely secular" celebration, designed basically for children. True, the holiday had a strikingly religious origin, but it is unrealistic to think that that tradition can be restored in all of its pristine innocence. Our culture does not warrant such hope. We are a different people at a different time. As a family, though, we can capitalize on what has become a customary secular ritual and help our children enjoy a sense of the sacred in this seemingly profane ritual. If we could send the goblins and witches, the Spider Men and Women, Draculas, the rabbits and princesses of the family into the streets on Halloween with just a morsel of that realization, then they would indeed have something to parade through town about. And the materialistic treats offered by the elders of the community would have more than sugar-coated significance.

On the following pages are some suggested family rituals. Feel free to modify them for your purposes and your family. Or use them as a springboard for designing your own rituals.

Creating a ritual demands that it be suited to the experiences and character of the participants. Only those aspects of them should be used that spark ideas and possibilities for your family.

Many families have their own rituals and experiences, perhaps generations old, that are much more valuable than the ones I suggest. These should be continued and also shared with other families.

In addition, to promote family fun days, one day each month should be set aside for the family to do something special together. Family fun days can be as beneficial as specific family religious activities. It is important to help families realize this. Going to a film, an outing, a museum, or just staying home around the fireplace with popcorn are as holy a time for families to share as going to church. Such fun events can help families see the relationship between faith and life in very special ways.

At the risk of repeating myself, the best rituals will be simple, natural, fun, and include time for sharing a food treat afterwards. Nothing attracts children like food treats, and ending an activity in that way builds anticipation to have a similar activity again. Besides, it is often over food, when everyone is relaxed, that the best sharing takes place.

In short, the bottom line is to remember your own family traditions and rituals. Look first at your own family and identify its traditions and rituals. Then look through the suggested rituals on the following pages and perhaps supplement or revise what you are now doing and incorporate some new rituals into your family's faith life.

PART II

FAMILY RITUALS:
CELEBRATING THE SEASONS

Advent to Christmas

Christmas is the celebration of the Gift of Emmanuel—God-in-this-world. The vibrancy and excitement of this precious gift is present to us only if we strive to help one another be aware of this in our families. Cel-ebrations recall root meanings and make truth present to us in a special way.

The "specialness" of Advent has always been that time spent waiting for the new presence of God at Christmas. The time we wait, then, is symbolic of the many occasions in life in which we must wait, yearn, and antici-pate a new birth—the experience of encountering Jesus anew.

Celebrating Advent in Your Home

Here are four things to decide first, for keeping Advent in your home:

1. During the week before Advent, get together and decide what your family will do together during Advent. Decide to-gether. Plan realistically. Be selective and concentrate on do-ing one or two activities well.

2. Have a definite date and time to begin. The first Sunday of Advent is best. Begin with a special prayer as well as your decided activities.

3. Be committed to the family decision and make it a prior-ity. The whole point is not to get so busy that Advent gets crowded out. Put it first.

4. Be careful not to let the Festival of Christmas interfere with the keeping of Advent.

A Family Advent Wreath

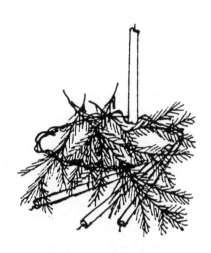

One of the best known customs for the season of Advent is the old German practice of the Advent Wreath. Although it has no direct liturgical significance, this wreath of evergreens with four blue candles is rich in symbolism which can make Advent more meaningful.

The *wreath* (a circle of evergreens) is a symbol of God and eternity—with no beginning and no end. The *evergreen color* represents hope, the hope we all have of eternal life and of Christ's coming into our lives and of our accepting him more completely. The *four candles* represent the four weeks of Advent and the thousands of years that the world waited for the Redeemer. *Candles* symbolize Christ the Light, who dispels the darkness by showing us the way.

Gather the family together on the Saturday evening before the first Sunday of Advent to assemble and bless the Advent Wreath. Explain the symbolism of each part of the wreath as the family puts it together.

The Blessing

Parent: People waited for thousands of years for the Christ whom God had promised. Each year the church uses the four weeks before Christmas to remember the long years of darkness when there wasn't Jesus. Our Advent wreath is a reminder to us that the birth of Jesus is Emmanuel, God-with-us, sharing our lives. His life is light to show us the way. It is also a reminder to us that we must work at preparing our hearts for Jesus to come into them once again.

All: O God, send your blessing upon our wreath and help us to understand its symbolism so that we might use it to help prepare our hearts for the coming of Christ.

After the blessing, the presiding parent says the prayer for the first week of Advent and invites another member of the family to light the first candle. Each week a different prayer is said and another candle is lighted so that by the fourth week of Advent all the candles are burning brightly.

First Week: God, I know what it's like to want something and wait for it. I've wanted so many things...and then after I got them I was happy for a little while, but, after all, they were just things and soon my happiness disappeared. Help me this Christmas, to want to be like Jesus, your son, so that instead of wanting and waiting for a lot of new things, I will be looking for ways to grow more loving, kind, and just. *All*: Amen.

Second Week: God, I believe that you have come into the world and that you want to come into my heart. I also believe that once I let you into my heart that you are present in the world today through me. Help me to remember to bring you wherever I go. *All*: Amen.

Third Week: God, I know that this is a season of hope. Help me to be the kind of person who radiates joy because I believe in your faithful presence. Give me hope and confidence in myself to go out and make your business my business. *All*: Amen.

Fourth Week: God, this year help me to do more than just sing all the familiar Christmas carols; help me to live them. You sent Jesus as a bond of peace between us. May that peace on earth begin with me, and may joy in the world shine through us, as a family. *All*: Amen.

(These are only suggested prayers, you may want to express your own faith by composing your own prayers.)

On Christmas Eve with your family, renew the evergreens. Add Christmas balls, or red and white carnations and replace the blue candles with white ones to symbolize Christ, the Light of the World who came to be with us. Or, use the idea of the Christ candle, also found in this section.

Family Advent Tree

Find a strong tree branch. Secure it in a pot of clay or sand, and cover the base with greens. Each day of Advent, spend a few moments with the Scriptures and find a verse that speaks of the coming of Christ or Messiah. Write the verse on a construction paper ornament (star, bell, etc.). Punch a hole in the ornament and run a piece of string or yarn through it. Each night, read the verse and then tie the verse/ornament to the tree.

The Jesse Tree

The *Jesse Tree* is a small evergreen tree or just a leafless branch on which symbols are placed which represent those who in the course of salvation history helped prepare the way for the Messiah or who were part of Christ's genealogy. The symbols start at the bottom of the tree and progress in relative chronological order.

Children love the Christmas tree, and making a Jesse Tree at home helps calm the impatience for a Christmas tree. A good family project for the second Sunday of Advent would be to make the symbols and trim a Jesse Tree. Symbols can be made from construction paper, felt, contact or wrapping paper over cardboard forms, or baker's dough. Make the Jesse Tree trimming a family ritual. Have members of the family make and hang one or more of the symbols and explain the symbol as they hang it on the tree. The ritual can be concluded with a prayer of blessing for the tree and the family by one of the parents. In the weeks that follow before Christmas, the family might spend time each day discussing the Bible stories that correspond to the symbols on the tree.

The symbols for the Jesse Tree are many and varied, but the most usual are the following:

The *Apple* symbolizes Adam and Eve to whom the promise of the Messiah was first made. This was the beginning of our salvation history.

The *Altar of Sacrifice* symbolizes the story of Abraham and Isaac. God established a covenant with Abraham and his descendants. "I will make my covenant between you and me, and will give you many children," God told Abraham. "I will give you and your children this land in which you live, and I will be your God." So this was God's part of the bargain, and from the chosen people God asked only love.

The *Ark*—The Chosen People were aware of the promise of the Messiah. They were also aware of the covenant of God to Abraham. For many years they kept the covenant faithfully. But as time went on, the people forgot the covenant and returned to evil ways. To remind them of their agreement, God sent a flood that destroyed all except the just man, Noah, and his family.

The *Coat of Many Colors* represents Joseph, the favorite son of Jacob, who was sold into slavery by his brothers, but who, like the Messiah, saved his brothers from death.

The people continued falling in and out of love with their God. To reestablish his covenant, God gave Moses *Tablets* of stone on which were written specific laws of Love.

The *Key and the Crown* represent King David. The prophets told that the Messiah would be of the House of David. He would be the key that opened heaven for all humankind.

A *Scroll* can represent the numerous prophets who continually reminded the people of the covenant Yahweh had made with them, and of the promise of the Messiah. It was through the prophets' tradition of constant correction and affirmation that there was a small remnant of people who accepted the Messiah.

The *Shell and Water* represent John the Baptist, the precursor of the Messiah and last of the Messianic prophets. John preached a baptism of repentance to help the people prepare for the Messiah.

St. Joseph, the foster father of Jesus, is represented by the *Hammer and Square* because he was a carpenter. Sometimes a *Donkey* is used to represent Joseph, because he led the donkey bearing Mary to Bethlehem.

The *Lily* is a symbol for Mary, the Mother of the Messiah.

The *chi-rho* (☧) is placed at the top of the tree to symbolize the Messiah or the Christ, the fulfillment of the promise and the "Desired one of all." *Chi* (x) and *rho* (P) are the first two Greek letters in the title *Christ*. (*Christ* is the Greek equivalent of the Hebrew title *Messiah*, meaning the Anointed One.)

Gift Certificate Tree

Children like to make presents for their families. A gift certificate or ticket tree is a simple way to inspire deeds of kindness as gifts children of any age can give.

Find a bare tree branch with several outgrowths. Secure it in a decorated tin can filled with clay or sand. During Advent, members of the family make specially shaped tickets for other

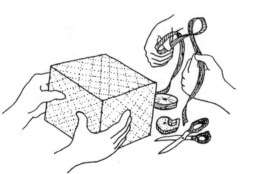

members of the family and hang the tickets with yarn on the tree branches.

On one side of the ticket, print the recipient's name; on the opposite side, print something that will be done for that person, e.g., take the other person's turn at doing dishes, make someone's bed, take out the garbage, polish the other person's shoes, etc. The gift is actually given when the recipient returns the ticket to the one who gave it.

This idea shows that gift-giving is more than just a "Christmas thing" and also emphasizes that a true gift represents part of the giver.

Life-Giving Gifts for the Christmas List

You might give similar gift certificates of service from your family to relatives, neighbors, friends. Sit down as a family and draw up your Christmas List—decide some personal way you might express the spirit of Christmas—giving the gift of self out of love. Design gift certificates indicating your family's gift. For example:

Dear_____,

Our family's Christmas present is running errands that you will need on slippery, cold days—or any days. Just call us at_____ after school. Merry Christmas.

Here are a few other ideas:

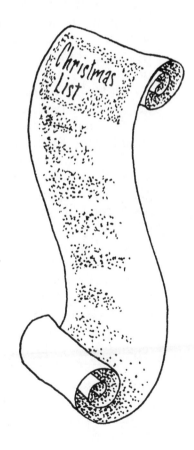

1. Give gifts of your own creating: candles, carving, needlepoint. Libraries and bookstores are loaded with books on crafts—even making things from junk.

2. Give a plant and directions for its care.

3. Give a service: a promise of so many hours of babysitting, a room painted, a garden planted, a car washed, a music lesson, an evening learning the names of the stars.

4. Give a gift of yourself: a story you have learned to tell, a dance or a song, a wonderful recipe.

5. Give parents or brothers and sisters something of the family: maybe a memento of some event.

6. Give a gift to the earth: begin to recycle all your paper, cans and bottles at a recycling center.

7. Donate money to a cause your friend is devoted to, and make the gift in the friend's name.

8. Save all your Christmas cards and send them back to the same people next year, asking them to do the same the following year, each time with a new date and message. It would be a tremendous historical memory in ten years!

9. Lend your car to a carless person once a week for a month or two. Or, offer to drive someone to work with you.

St. Nicholas Day—December 6

Nicholas was a kindly and popular bishop who lived in the fourth century. Although he tried to perform his acts of kindness in secret, he became known for his generosity, taking care of orphans, giving dowries to poor servant girls, dropping money down chimneys for the poor families to use, leaving food outside doors of hungry people. After his death, his kindnesses became legend in the minds and hearts of the needy. When he was declared a saint, his feast day was set on December 6, and the day became an occasion for gift-giving, especially to children. The custom in many European (and American) families is to have the children (big and small) leave their empty shoes outside their doors in hopes that some "unknown visitor" will fill them up, with oranges, apples, foil-covered chocolate "coins," or real ones, gifts given for no particular reason. Nicholas himself supposedly dispatched his gifts in shoes and stockings. He is patron saint of Russia and Greece.

The idea of Santa Claus is often traced to St. Nicholas, but it is also mingled with a non-religious, Germanic legend about Thor, the kindly god of fire, who was associated with yule logs, fires and winter, and who rode in a chariot drawn by goats named Cracker and Gnasher.

On December 5, the eve of St. Nicholas Day, explain the legend and follow through by having the children (and adults) put out shoes. Then, perhaps, each member of the family could decide on something to give away to someone else on December 6, not just because it's getting near the Christmas season, but because someone has need of what you have.

Origins of Christmas Traditions

The Date

The first reference to the feast of Christmas is found in the Roman chronograph of A.D. 354, an almanac copied and illustrated by the Greek artist, Philocalus. This document contains a rudimentary Christian calendar in the form of two sets of dates.

At the head of the first set, for December 25, we find "Birth of Christ in Bethlehem of Judea." The date of December 25 was deliberately chosen at Rome sometime between A.D. 274 and 336 in order to counter the pagan feast of "Sol Invictus," the Unconquerable Sun, a feast which was officially instituted in 274 by the Emperor Aurelian.

From an anonymous treatise dating from the third or early fourth century, we read "...now they call this day the *Birthday of the Unconquerable!*" Who indeed is so unconquerable as our Savior, who overthrew and conquered death? And as for talking about the birthday of the Sun! He is the Sun of Justice! He of whom the prophet Malachi said, "For you who fear my name there will arise the Sun of Justice, with healing wings."

The Paradise Tree

Hanging ornaments on trees seems to go all the way back to Roman times. Decorating a "Christmas Tree," however, seems to date from the 16th century in Germany. There, evergreen branches were freighted down with apples, sugar candy, and painted nuts. The inspiration for the "Christmas Tree" came from the medieval "mystery plays," performed in churches during the middle ages. A yearly favorite was an Advent performance called the "Paradise Play"—humankind's creation, expulsion from Eden, and promise of a savior. The only prop on stage was a fir tree, with apples suspended from its branches. Eventually the tree found its way into Christian homes. Later on, to point out to their children that the "paradise tree" was no longer a symbol of sin, but a symbol of salvation, 16th century Germans combined it with another ancient symbol, The "Christmas Light." They also began to hang candles and cookies along side the "apples of sin" to symbolize the grace of "salvation." Thus, the "tree of sin," and the "light of Christ" grew into the *tree of light*, with its salvation-symbols. Today we all call it the "Christmas tree."

Christmas Cards

A little over 100 years ago, a wallpaper designer, Louis Prang of Boston, put on sale the first Christmas cards. However, the practice had been going on in England for at least 20 years before Prang. The first engraved Christmas cards showed up in London in 1842. Today, over 5 billion cards bulge the postcarrier's bag each December. If you send Christmas cards, consider waiting until after Christmas, not only to give the postcarrier a break, but to allow Advent its own time and celebration.

The Christmas Crèche

Crèche is a French word meaning "cradle." It has been part of the Christmas tradition for over 750 years. The nativity scene was popularized as a Christmas custom by St. Francis of Assisi in 1224. St. Francis erected a manger and acted out the first Christmas with a cast of characters that included live animals and real people.

Homemade Crèche Figures

Making your own nativity figures for a crèche can be both simple and enjoyable, and is an excellent way to review the Christmas story with children.

Collect all the pieces of cloth that have been stashed away for months. Make a water and flour solution (make it watery, not pastey). Use a styrofoam cone shape for the body of each figure; use an egg-shaped styrofoam ball for each head. Soak the pieces of material in the flour solution—*do not wring*. Then gently drape the wet material over the cone. This can be done in layers. Head pieces can be added, or decorative beads, sequins, etc. while the material is still wet, or they can be glued on after it has dried. Do not move the figures until the material is completely dry (usually 24 hours). The result is a crèche unique to your family that can be used year after year.

"Magical" Mistletoe

Cutting the mistletoe was once an occasion of great solemnity. Druid priests headed a stately procession into the forest to the site of the chosen oak. (Mistletoe grows on oak trees.) The Arch-Druid, robed all in white, climbed the tree and cut down the sacred vine with a golden sickle. Young maidens caught the mistletoe in a fair cloth, spread out below for that purpose. Then the mistletoe was divided, and each family bore home a sprig to hang over the door, for they believed that the powers of the plant to cure and to protect were very great. Indeed, according to legend, warring parties which met under mistletoe were said to have been overcome by its power, so that they would lay down their weapons and depart friends.

The English called the mistletoe "allheal"; the Welsh, "guidhel." Mistletoe later was used in Christian homes as a symbol of Christ, the divine healer. Today we kiss under the mistletoe.

Mexican Luminaria

The Mexican Luminaria is a simply made, inexpensive, energy-saving, yet attractive Christmas lawn decoration, as well as a meaningful custom.

The Luminaria consists of a medium-sized brown or other-colored bag with about an inch and a half of sand in the bottom. A votive-size candle is set in the sand.

Instead of a paper bag you can make the Luminaria from a larger juice can. Simply fill the cans with water, freeze, remove from freezer and with a nail and hammer "punch out" appropriate designs. After ice has melted and been emptied out, add sand or small stones and a votive candle as in bag.

Several of these are made to line the sidewalk and steps to the front door on Christmas Eve night as a sign of room and hospitality to Mary and Joseph, and to anyone who might be alone or traveling on this night.

The Christ Candle

The Christ Candle is a beautiful symbol of Jesus, the Light of the World. It is made by using a tall two-inch candle and decorating it with a chi-rho and other symbols of Christ painted on the candle with acrylics or nail polish.

A good day to make the Christ Candle would be December 8, the Feast of the Immaculate Conception. When the decorating is completed, place the candle in a holder and cover it with a blue mantle, symbolic of Mary. On Christmas Day remove the mantle and light the candle.

The Miracle of the Poinsettia

The poinsettia was named after Dr. Joel Roberts Poinsett, who served as United States Ambassador to Mexico. Upon his return in 1829, he brought this flower with him to his home in South Carolina, where it flourished.

The people of Mexico call the poinsettia "The Flower of the Holy Night." According to a legend, on Christmas Eve long ago, a poor little boy went to church in great sadness, because he had no gift to bring to the holy child. He dared not enter the church; and kneeling humbly on the ground, he prayed and assured God how much he wanted to offer some lovely present. "But I am very poor and dread to approach you with empty hands." When he finally rose from his knees, there, springing up where his tears had fallen, was a green plant, with gorgeous blooms of dazzling red.

The poinsettia is today the traditional flower of Christmastide.

Celebrating Hanukkah

Like Christmas, Hanukkah has its origins in the change that happens to the sun during this season. And, like Christmas, Hanukkah has its historic occasion. In the second century before Jesus, the Jewish brothers Maccabees led a victorious revolt against the foreign occupiers of the land and were able to reclaim and rededicate the temple in Jerusalem (the word *Hanukkah* means "dedication").

The legend says that when the temple was recaptured, all of the sacred oil had been profaned except for a one day supply. It would take eight days to sanctify new oil. But a miracle happened and a tiny bit of holy oil burned for the whole eight days.

In the Jewish tradition, Hanukkah is a home festival. The simple observance of Hanukkah in the home can be occasion for a household to pray together.

A Simple Ritual
for the Evenings of Hanukkah

The ritual calls for a nine-branched candleholder and 44 small candles (3 1/2" birthday candles will work well). Make your own candelabra (called *menorah* in Hebrew) out of spools attached to a base, tinkertoys assembled in a variety of ways, clay, a piece of driftwood with nine holes drilled into it, etc.

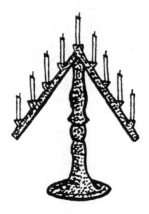

Hanukkah lasts eight days: one candle is lighted the first day, two the second, etc. The ninth hole in the menorah is for the "servant candle" which lights the others each night. The reason for the small candles is that, by one custom, the lights are allowed to burn out each night. While this happens, nothing is done except to watch, to pray, and to enjoy the light, the darkness, and the quiet.

The Service

Light the "servant candle" and recite the blessings:

Blessed are you, Lord our God, ruler of the universe. You have given us life and permitted us to reach this season.

Blessed are you, Lord our God, ruler of the universe. You have sanctified us with your commandments and commanded us to kindle the light of Hanukkah.

Blessed are you, Lord our God, ruler of the universe. You performed miracles for our ancestors in those days, at this season.

Then the candle(s) are lighted and another member of the family says:

> We kindle these lights on account of the miracles, wonders, and deliverances which you performed for our ancestors. These lights are sacred throughout the eight days of Hanukkah; we are not permitted to make any use of them, but only to look at them, in order to give thanks to you.

A simple song after this would be good, e.g., a verse of "O Come, O Come, Emmanuel" or "Prepare Ye" from *Godspel*.

In silence, let the candles burn out and then remain silent for a few moments in the dark.

Although not a usual part of the service, your family might wish to add a Scripture reading each evening. The following schedule introduces a different prophet each evening and serves to bring a note of the Advent season into Hanukkah:

First night: Amos 5:14-15
Second night: Josea 2:18-20
Third night: Joel 3:1-3
Fourth night: Jeremiah 33:14-16
Fifth night: Isaiah 7:14
Sixth night: Ezekiel 37:1-14
Seventh night: Isaiah 40:3-5
Eighth night: Malachi 3:1

Pre-Christmas Activities

Begin some of your own traditions with your family. Here are a few examples:

Shopping for Fun

Take the whole family to a shopping center, not to buy anything, but just for fun. Watch the people. Look at the decorations. What are people buying? What are their moods? How many are using credit cards? What is the most unusual thing that you see? Do some people look like Scrooge? Are children's eyes bigger and brighter than usual?

On the way home, stop somewhere for hot chocolate and talk over what each in the family has observed and share reactions.

Christmas Goodies
Choose a baking day in which everyone participates. Everyone likes to eat Christmas goodies, so everyone ought to have a part in making them. And while the family is busy baking together, you can have a family caroling session.

Television Party
Even though many people are unhappy with the quality of television programming, there are some exceptionally good opportunities. Why not check the TV schedule in search of a Christmas special the family can view together? Plan popcorn or something special for the evening.

Blessing for the Family
The Feast of the Holy Family (December 30) would be a good day to pray this blessing. You will need a bowl of water and a lighted candle.

Parent: Thank you, God, for making us an ordinary family with ordinary problems and joys. We don't seek the model marriage, the brightest children or the best neighborhood. We are content with the gifts your have given us. (*Name some of them*.) For these we thank you, Lord. Let your light shine through our ordinariness. Amen.

Each person, beginning with parent(s) now dips his or her thumb into the bowl of water, traces the sign of the cross on the forehead of each family member and says: "May God bless you and keep you safe."

Blessing for Family Members Living Away: children, grandparents, aunts, uncles, cousins, etc.

Bless (*name them*) living to the north of us, God, keep them in your care.

(*Sprinkle water toward the north.*)

Bless (N.N.) living to the south of us, God, keep them in your care.

(*Sprinkle water toward the south.*)

Bless (N.N.) living to the east of us, God, keep them in your care.

(*Sprinkle water toward the east.*)

Bless (N.N.) living to the west of us, God, keep them in your care.

(*Sprinkle water toward the west.*)

Join hands around the candle and water and pray the Lord's Prayer.

Christmas to Epiphany

Christmas Eve Prayer Service
The whole family might plan this special service of hymns, Scripture readings and prayers for Christmas Eve. It is not difficult to choose appropriate readings and songs for this occasion. The service might take place just before opening gifts or after dinner.

Blessing the Crêche

In a small procession, each household member can carry one of the crêche figures to its place of honor. When all the figures are in place, a parent can proceed with the prayer of blessing:

> God of Love, bless this crêche we have prepared in remembrance of the birth of your Son. We ask that the light of Christ's goodness shine on all of us here.

Sprinkle the crêche with holy water; incense may also be used.

Blessing for the Tree

> God of Life and Light, we ask your blessing upon this tree. May its ever-greenness be a sign in our lives of the hope of the Christmas season, its glittering ornaments a sign of the joy of the Christmas season, and the gifts beneath it a sign of the love of the Christmas season.

Sprinkle the tree with holy water. Conclude this little ritual by bringing its significance home to the present day. Discuss the following questions with one another:

- What if Jesus were born now? How would the holy family look?
- Where would the baby be born? Think of the places that would be like Bethlehem—no room, a stable, and a manger.
- Imagine who would be like angels, shepherds, sheep, the Wise Men.
- Are there people as evil and powerful as King Herod and his counselors? Who are they?

Blessing of the Christmas Dinner

If you already have a tradition for blessing this meal, then by all means continue it. If you do not, the following may help you get started.

The stuff of which this blessing is made is the love that went into the selection and preparation of the food, the generosity of those who labored that such food might be purchased, the beauty of the table which has been set, perhaps the labor of making special place markers. But most of all, the blessing is in the fellowship of the table, the gathering itself, and the time we take for this. Let nothing be hurried. The blessing begins when all have assembled at the table. The ringing of a small jingle bell might call everyone to silence. Then in silence the oldest child lights the candles. When they are burning, one of the adults prays:

> For the wonder of birth, we thank you, God. And for this day to celebrate the birth of Jesus at Bethlehem, we sing with the angels, with the cattle and the sheep, with the shepherds and the stars of heaven, with Joseph and Mary:

All join hands and sing: "O Come Let Us Adore Him! O Come Let Us Adore Him! O Come Let Us Adore Him, Christ the Lord."

The leader continues after all have taken their glasses (of water, wine, milk, or whatever) and are holding them for a toast:

> May your blessing, O God, be upon all creation. May the earth that brought forth this food be blessed, and all of us. May the first banquet of this holy season be a sharing of the meal that happened at Bethlehem when in Jesus' birth you shared with your own holiness.

Then all say a "Merry Christmas" and drink together. This blessing might be used for festive meals throughout the

Christmas season: simply add in the first prayer...The birth of Jesus at Bethlehem, the House of Bread, and the holiness of his friend, John the apostle...or...and the glory of his manifestation to the Magi....

Keeping Christmas Rituals
for the Twelve Days After Christmas

How has it ever happened that Christmas can be over and gone, totally wiped out, by the morning of December 26? Or even by the afternoon of December 25 in some cases?

Christmas is a *season*—not just a day—lasting 12 days. In fact, in most European countries the gift-giving aspect of the season takes place on Epiphany, the Feast of the Magi's visit when Jesus' birth was revealed to the Gentile (non-Jewish) nations. December 25 is reserved for the celebration of Christ's birth. It might be good for us to save some of our gift-giving for Epiphany, since Christmas so often seems to end when the last package is unwrapped.

We need to make the Christmas season a festival, a time when business-as-usual stops, a time when we tell special stories. Now the story of Christmas is the most out-of-the-ordinary story of a birth. But like all good stories, this birth story surrounds itself with other stories that seem to overflow. If we are to make Christmas a season, then we need to place the story, and that is the purpose of this section of the book.

If we believe there is a reason for festivity, then *we* make the festival by being willing to take the time and energy to do the unusual; for example, leave your tree up until January 6 (Epiphany), go caroling on the feast of St. Stephen (December 26), etc.

As with your Advent planning, gather the household together for Christmas planning, remembering, futuring. Encourage children to recall and tell what they remember about past Christmases. What was most fun, exciting, beautiful? Parents, too, recall sad times, high points, customs, foods. How did the grandparents celebrate Christmas? What has changed? What has stayed the same? What about Christmas this year? What's good and holy? What's bad and selfish? How shall we celebrate it? Make a short list of suggestions (things to keep, things to drop, things to leave the same); look at them again on Epiphany, and the next year. See if you feel the same.

New Year's Eve

How about three or four families gathering together on New Year's Eve to share fun, frolic, food, prayer, and to welcome in the New Year?

The morning can be spent sleeping in, of course. Each family might share brunch and then gather with the other families for an afternoon of sledding, hiking, cross-country or downhill skiing, swimming, skating, movie-going, whatever. The evening meal can be pot luck or each family might bring a favorite soup with the host family providing a salad and desert. After eating, the time can be spent playing games, telling stories, or just visiting.

As midnight approaches, all gather with each family having the previous year's calendar. Beginning with January of that year, share the happy and sad memories of each month. When all have shared something of the month, that month's page is torn from each family's calendar and burned, or crumpled if there is no safe way to burn it.

After the old year is remembered, family resolutions for the new year are made and perhaps written on the new family calendar as a reminder. At the stroke of midnight, families wish each other peace, joy, and blessings for the year ahead.

The following New Year's Day Prayer can be prayed together before all depart for home.

New Year's Day Prayer

> Lord,
> As we begin this year we pray anew
> Forgive our forgettings
> Melt our hostilities
> Give us the courage to begin again.
> Make our memories stronger
> That we might forget less
> Forgive more

Grow in relationships
Reach out further
Show our care
Hurry less
Take the time to do those things
that count the most.
Help us remember
That we need to do this especially
With those who are dearest
Families
Friends
Neighbors
Those who shape our lives and our days.
Keep us peaceful and just
Kind and compassionate
Gentle and generous
Filled with the Light of your love. Amen.

A New Year's custom that deserves ritual is taking this day to visit friends: old friends and new, announced and unannounced visits. Bring along a big bag of nuts (some will think that appropriate for anyone who would not spend New Year's Day before the TV) to share with your friends and with those you meet on the way (try walking!).

An Epiphany Celebration
January 6 is the day we celebrate the Magi finally reaching the crêche. Until that time, children can have great fun moving them a few inches across the room until the great day that they arrive, and Christ is made manifest to the Gentiles.

Have the children help make a "crown cake" (bundt cakes can give the illusion of a crown topped with frosting and gum-drop jewels). This will help the family to see that the gifts brought by the Magi (who were astrologers of sorts) were recognizing Christ's kingship.

An evening re-enactment of the story of the Magi can also be a most enjoyable experience, since children love to dramatize things. To begin the enactment, someone can read the Scripture account of Jesus' manifestation (Matthew 2:1-12). Then have family members assume the roles of Herod, the Magi. (It is not necessary to have exactly three, since there probably were not three; there may have been two, six, or any number of them.) They meet and talk to Herod and finally reach Bethlehem where Mom, Dad, and the baby of the family (Jesus was probably two years old), or a doll, are playing the roles of Mary, Joseph, and Jesus. The gifts presented might be resolutions written on paper in boxes beautifully wrapped as gifts. When the dramatization is over, share the "crown cake" together.

Ash Wednesday to Easter

Lenten Activities at Home
Lent is a time of prayer, penance and sacrifice, a time for the entire family to be more attentive to the words of Jesus and to each other. It is a time to try harder to put Christ's teachings into practice. It is a time of concentrated effort toward the springtime of spiritual growth, of rebirth and renewal.

However, the perennial problem in families seems to be: How can our children best experience the 40 days of Lent? How can they learn the real meaning of sacrifice?

Following are a number of activities you might try to aid in an experiential celebration of the season and a means whereby the problem might begin to be worked out for your family. You may wish to choose one or more of the suggestions.

Forty days is a very long time for children. To have Lent become more meaningful for them, take one week and perhaps one activity at a time. However, family prayer could be continued throughout the season and after.

Regarding sacrifice: A child is capable of real sacrifice, but the beauty of such sacrifice is its spontaneity; at such times one feels the Spirit of God at work. To suggest that a child "give something up" or do something nice for someone because it pleases Jesus actually tampers with his or her early moral development. If the child would like to do something kind for someone, that is *sufficient in itself* as an act that makes the child more Christ-like and as an attempt to follow the teaching of the gospel. Lent is a journey *with* Jesus, not *for* him.

Ash Wednesday Family Service

Seasons like Lent need a definite beginning. All good resolutions go into effect today. If the whole family can't get to the church for the service, have a prayer service at home. Ashes can be made out of things or symbols of things that you want to bring under control in your life, e.g., money, faults written on paper, etc.

Gather the family together, read and discuss Joel 2:12-18 or Matthew 6:1-6, 16-18. Allow a few minutes for thought during which each member of the family decides which faults will be worked on. These are written on a small piece of paper, crumpled and placed in a brazier to be burned with last year's palm branch. You might also cut a hunk of hair from each person's head to be burned. Set a fire and watch as part of you is turned quickly to ashes. As the fire burns, the parent says: "God, have mercy on us, forgive us, and help us to do better in the future." Then stand in silence until the flame dies out.

While the contents of the brazier are cooling, the family might discuss the meaning of Lent and what each person or the household as a whole is going to do to grow during the season.

When the ashes are cool, the oldest takes some and marks the forehead of the next oldest saying: "Repent and receive the Good News..."and so through the entire family until the youngest marks the oldest. The service can be concluded with a song or prayer together.

A Lenten Journey of Love

We are a pilgrim people, and while Lent is a good time to look back on where we have been, more importantly, we look ahead toward where we are going. This *Journey of Love* may be an aid. It was originated several years ago by the pastor of the First Christian Church in Oklahoma City. For each of the six weeks of Lent, there are specific aspects of daily loving.

First Week: The Hand of Love. Write a letter a day to a friend near or far away and tell him or her how much you appreciate their friendship.

 *Second Week: The voice of Love.* Phone two or three people just to say what they mean to you or to say "Thank you" or "I'm sorry." Call people you've intended to phone but somehow never have. Remember, love and gossip don't go together.

Third Week: The Deed of Love. Take something you have made or bought to two or three friends who mean much to you, but for whom you rarely express your love—a pie, a plant, a birdhouse, a small remembrance that has your love as a wrapping.

 Fourth Week: The Heart of Love. Make a list of ten people for whom you will pray daily. Include your friends, your enemies, those you don't like. Forgive them if they have wronged you, and ask forgiveness if you have wronged them.

Fifth Week: The Mind of Love. Use this week to pray for yourself and look inward. Read the gospel of John. Plan during the week to do a little extra meditating and praying in a quiet place, such as a church.

Sixth Week: The Victory of Love. This is the week of celebration. God's love for us is revealed in many ways. Get out of doors and breathe in the air of spring. Fly a kite. Have your friends in for dinner or a party. Let your joy be full with life abundant in faith, hope, and love.

This little plan for Lent could well find us at Easter, a "new creation." And some, if not all, our faults could well turn to ashes and dust as we are reminded on Ash Wednesday. Their ash becomes a sign of victory through forgiveness. It is a journey of love which may entail some pain and difficulty—but aren't these basic ingredients of loving?

Goodbye to Alleluia

By ancient custom, the *Alleluia* is not spoken or sung during Lent. Some say that's silly: it's just a word in Hebrew that means "Praise the Lord!" We say it in English, why not in Hebrew? But *Alleluia* is more than a word. It's a part of who we are. Our ancestors in the faith have shouted it since long before Jesus.

At one time, it was customary for Christians to bury the *Alleluia* before Lent. We can revive the practice. With another family or two, form a procession, carrying spades, an empty wooden box, a beautiful *Alleluia* on paper or fabric (made by the children). Go to the largest snowdrift in the yard (the one that will melt the slowest) and dig a deep grave, then sing a last, most enthusiastic *Alleluia*. The written *Alleluia* is then placed in its coffin and buried as every-one takes a turn throwing on snow. Then join hands and pray for a good Lent and that all other seeds to be buried in the weeks ahead will sing their *Alleluias*. The *Alleluia* is raised on Easter with song and flowers.

Lenten Calendar

Make an appropriately decorated calendar of the 40 days of Lent by superimposing two pieces of heavy paper. For each day have a flap that opens to the back sheet to reveal an activity for the family for that day. For example: reading a particular Bible story, praying a decade of the rosary, visiting a nursing home, sharing cookies or cake with a neighbor, sharing allowances, fasting at one meal and giving the money saved to a social action agency or some other charity, etc.

For Under 18 Only

Lent means *doing something* more than *giving up* something. Is there something from the following list that you could try to *do* during Lent, completely on your own, without your parents "making you" do it?

•You know that neighbor on the block whom no one likes? Find a way to be friendly. (OK, no one said this was going to be easy.)

•Read a bedtime story to your younger brothers and sisters.

•Shovel walks for someone who can't—without pay.

•Visit a lonely shut-in.

•Listen to someone you don't enjoy.

•Be a peacemaker with a younger brother or sister.

•Give Mom a hug when she's having a bad day.

•Smile more often to let others know that you want to share your happiness.

•Babysit for a mother who doesn't get out very often—without pay.

•Show your understanding side to a friend who is having a bad day.

•Teach a younger family member a new game, or play an old game with them.

•Make banners to remind the family that Easter is coming.

•Take a walk with someone in your family after supper or on a weekend.

•Read to a blind person.

•Add an extra "I love you" to your daily conversation at home.

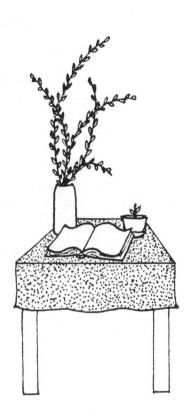

The Waiting Table

Watching and waiting are other characteristics of Lent. We wait for the new life of spring; for Easter, when we commemorate Christ's resurrection, and the special time when we can celebrate our new life in baptism. Lent is also a time of interior activity and growth.

Begin with a special trip to the store to find some purple fabric (purple is a lenten color) to be hemmed for a tablecloth. The Scriptures are placed in the center of the table. As Lent progresses, the table can be decorated first with dormant branches; then as the first signs of spring begin to show themselves, the branches can be replaced with daffodils, tulips, pussy willows, or lilac branches.

You might also experiment with indoor growing projects which the children can watch. Mustard, bean, wheat, or marigold seeds work well, as do sweet potatoes or carrot tops. As time goes on, children will begin to find objects which to them are symbolic of waiting for spring, and of the death-to-life activity taking place within nature.

Pictures depicting the events of Palm Sunday, Holy Thursday, and Good Friday, either drawn by the children or commercial pictures can be added at the appropriate times to depict Jesus' journey from death to new life. Pictures and mementos of the children's baptisms can also be added after a discussion of how Lent was a special time for the early Christians to prepare for their baptism, which was conferred at the Easter Vigil Service.

For Easter, the tablecloth is changed to white. A candle can be decorated with symbols of spring and Easter or with the symbols that are on the Paschal candle at church and given the place of honor next to the scriptures on the table, representing the Light of Christ Risen. Flowers, Easter eggs, butterflies, stuffed bunnies and chicks, and other symbols of spring and Easter can surround the candle and bible.

Personalized Cross

Make either a wooden cross (out of sticks or boards) or a paper cross to be tacked on the wall. Have each member of the family trace his or her hand on construction paper, cut it out and write on it something special that he or she would like to do during Lent (these can be changed weekly). The hands are then placed on the cross as a reminder. On Holy Saturday, remove the hands and replace them with tissue or crepe paper or silk flowers to show that the efforts to be better Christians during Lent turned into something beautiful, as did the glorious cross of Christ on the resurrection.

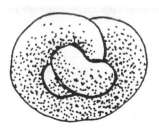

Pretzel Prayer Reminders

Making pretzels is an ancient lenten custom. Legend has it that one day a monk who made altar breads found himself with leftover dough. He shaped the dough into the form of dolls with arms crossed in prayer, went out into the streets and gave them to the children to remind them to pray. The breads were called *bracellae,* which means "little arms."

From this Latin word, the Germans later coined the word "pretzel." Lent is a time of prayer. And the pretzel is a reminder. How about the family making pretzels together during Lent?

Popcorn Project

A paper cup with appropriate lenten or spring decorations is placed in a special place, accessible to all. Next to it is a jar of popcorn kernels. Each day, each member of the family decides upon something to work on for that day. For example: trying to use the gift of their hands to help others, to share with others and to take care of things. The gift of ears to listen better to others; the gift of eyes to see the needs of others, to see the beauty of all God's creation and to keep their eyes on their own work. The gift of speech to thank God for God's many gifts, to be quiet at times so that others are able to learn or pray, to speak loudly enough so that others may hear, to speak only kindly of others, etc. For each good deed done, a kernel of corn is added to the cup. At the end of each week, the kernels can be popped and shared. Watching the kernels grow and burst and change can be a good symbol of how the little things done each day can bring about a growth in the Christ Life within us.

Progressive Butterfly Banner

The butterfly is an ancient Easter symbol. To visualize the lenten experience of death-resurrection, try a progressive butterfly banner. Just as the butterfly which emerges from the cocoon is the same caterpillar in new form, so Jesus, emerging from the tomb is the same person—glorified.

Take a piece of felt or large poster paper. Each week, add one part to the poster as follows: 1) a bare branch with a caption such as *Life Through Death*; 2) a cocoon on the branch; 3) a head is added to the cocoon which now becomes the body of the butterfly; 4) legs are added; 5) eyes are added to the head; 6) three-dimensional wings are added to complete the Easter poster. Adding to the poster can be done as part of your family prayer.

Family Food Box

At the end of dinner, there's a brief discussion about the next day's dinner menu. The cook tells what's planned. Then one of the family (depending on whose turn it is) decides which item on the menu to eliminate. The money that item would cost is then put in the family food box to be used to buy food for the hungry. For example, on the day spaghetti, salad and garlic bread are on the menu, the one whose turn it is to eliminate an item suggests, "Let's not have meat in the spaghetti sauce" and into the food box goes three dollars.

At the end of the lenten season, contribute the money to a cause of justice or mercy.

Passover Meal at Home

Celebrate a family Passover meal and enable the family to experience the relationship between our Jewish and Christian ritual heritage. Passover usually coincides with Holy Week. Holy Thursday would be a good day to have a family Passover, with a follow-up experience of the celebration of the institution of the eucharist. You may also wish to invite another family to celebrate with you.

Sometime during Lent, the story of the Israelites' exile, slaver, and liberation should be read or told with an explanation of the celebration of Passover as a Thanksgiving feast celebrated annually in honor of their freedom. Both Passover for the Jews and Easter for Christians recognize that all things come from God: light, bread, wine, freedom—all good things. The Jewish prayers are prayed in a spirit of thanksgiving and blessing, as are the Eucharistic Prayers. The Exodus celebrates the chosen people's freedom from oppression. Each Jew is to become aware of this personally at each Passover. For the Christian, the Paschal season celebrates redemption from the effects of sin by Christ's passion and resurrection, and God's gift of grace, especially through holy communion. Both are rooted in history and Scripture to show God's fulfillment of God's plan of salvation.

Passover Meal

The following is designed to assist you with the planning, preparation, and celebration of the Passover or Paschal meal. The Passover meal itself will run well over an hour, so plan to set aside a good portion of the evening for it. Members of the group who will be sharing the meal should be involved in the preparation of the meal. This will probably mean that you will want to begin early with preparations, even a day or two in advance.

Preparation:

1. *House Cleaning*: Members of the family join in the task of house cleaning. On the afternoon or the day before the meal, have several members clean area(s) to be used for the meal. The setting up of tables and chairs, plates, cups, etc., is all a part of this house-cleaning ritual and should be part of the day's preparation.

2. *Decorations*: This ritual meal is rich with symbolism; ideas for decorations are unlimited. Table decorations, centerpieces, wall hangings, place cards, and many other items can be made by the family based upon the predominant symbols of the ritual. The making of such decoration can be part of the afternoon's or week's preparations and will serve to enhance the ritual meal.

To add to the solemnity of the meal, participants can dress up in formal attire for the meal.

3. *The Passover Foods: The Menu*

Roast Lamb—to symbolize the sacrificial lamb offered by

the Israelites and eaten on the eve of their departure from Egypt. In the Christian tradition, the Lamb of God is a symbol of Jesus Christ.

Matzos—to symbolize the unleavened bread the Jews ate when they were freed from Egypt. Available at the market. It can also be made using the following recipe:

3 cups whole wheat or rye flour
1 tsp. salt
1 tblsp. brown sugar or honey
1 1/4 cup sour milk
1 egg
1/2 cup melted butter
1 tblsp. baking powder
Roll out 1/2 inch flat with rolling pin or hands on a floured surface and make into round forms.
Bake: 425° for 15 minutes.

Bitter Herbs—to symbolize the bitterness of slavery and addictions. Use horseradish or spring radishes.

Greens—As a token of gratitude to God for the products of the earth. Use parsley and watercress or endive.

Salt Water—A dip for the greens and bitter herbs.

Haroses—to symbolize the mortar which the Hebrew slaves used in their servitude. A mixture of chopped apples, chopped nuts, cinnamon and wine (this may be prepared like a fruit salad or chopped in a blender).

Wine—to symbolize the blood marking the doorposts of the Jews so that the avenging angel would pass over them. In Christian tradition, we commemorate the blood of Christ shed in his passion. Use preferably a red wine.

Additional Foods:
The traditional Passover menu may be supplemented with other foods to "fill out" the meal. Some possibilities are rice, a vegetable or green salad, and perhaps a cake for dessert. (A white coconut cake in the shape of a lamb would be very appropriate.)

If additional foods are to be used, they should not be

present at the table until the ritual meal has been eaten. The traditional Passover foods (above menu) should be present on the table from the beginning of the ritual (some lamb may be kept warm—the bone and small pieces may be on the table prior to the meal). These traditional foods, however, should not be consumed until the appropriate time in the ritual.

Notes on Passover Foods:

1. Be sure that enough of the Passover foods are available. When the ritual calls for the eating or drinking of a food, only a small portion need be taken by each person. The remainder of the food can be saved for later in the meal after the ritual section.

2. If young people are present, you may wish to dilute the wine with water, cherry Kool-Aid, or soda; or use a non-alcoholic wine.

3. The ceremonial cups of wine may be served in one of two ways:

Each person has his or her own glass of wine, or one large cup is used from which all can drink.

Additional Notes:

1. Please go through the ritual carefully before the meal so that you are familiar with the order of events, with pronunciation of words and with phrasing.

2. Feel free to make your own personal additions as you see appropriate for your group. But be sure to retain the significance of this very special meal.

3. Readers are needed for these reading parts: mother, leader, parent or grandparent, child.

The Ritual

I. Introductory Blessings

All gather around the table and stand quietly. The mother lights the candles and says the following traditional prayer of the mother in the Jewish family as she lights the festival day candle before the meal:

Mother: Blessed are you, O Lord God, King of the universe, who has sanctified us by your commandments and has commanded us to light the festival lights. Blessed are you, O Lord God, King of the universe, who has kept us alive and sustained us and brought us to this season. May our home be consecrated, O God, by the light of your countenance, shining upon us in blessing and bringing us peace.

Leader: This is Holy Week, a time that joins for us the Old and the New Covenant. At this season, the Jewish people celebrate the feast of the Passover or Pasch. More than 1400 years before the time of Jesus the Christ, the chosen people were suffering in slavery in Egypt. God raised up Moses as their leader, and Moses tried to secure their release from captivity. Despite the hardships of nine successive plagues that God sent to them, the Egyptian pharaoh still refused the pleas of Moses to set his people free. Then an angel of the Lord was sent to strike down the first-born son of every Egyptian family, but at God's command, each Jewish family had sacrificed a lamb and sprinkled its blood on the doorposts. And the angel, seeing the blood, passed over their homes and their children were spared.

Then, finally, the pharaoh permitted the Jews to leave because he feared further punishment. They fled in haste, to wander amid the hardships in the desert for 40 years before coming to the promised land of Israel. And God commanded Moses that the Jews should make a remembrance of their day of deliverance. Thus the Passover became the great feast of sacrifice, of deliverance and of thanksgiving. Each Passover meal revolves around the retelling (the *Haggadah*) of this providential act (see Exodus 12).

We who are the followers of Christ see the working of God's concern for the people of God. As God sent Moses to rescue the Israelites from captivity in Egypt, so God sent Jesus to lead humankind from slavery and sin. Through his life, death, and resurrection Christ enables us to enter life with God.

At this time, Christians and Jews celebrate their own feasts in their own ways, and we can see in these celebrations the common bond of the symbolism of the Exodus. Jesus was a Jew, and today we wish to draw upon the traditional Jewish Seder and the words of the New Testament to help us more fully appreciate Jesus' observance of his Jewish heritage, whose laws and rituals he kept.

Matthew's (26:17), Mark's (14:12), and Luke's (22:7-9) accounts of Jesus' passion and death for us each begin with his celebration of the Paschal meal: "Now on the first day of Unleavened Bread the disciples came to Jesus to say, 'Where do you want us to make the preparations for you to eat the Passover?'"

II. Introductory Hallel: Psalms of Praise

Leader: In the Passover feast, before the meal is eaten, the first psalms of the *Hallel*—the hymns of praise which the Jews recited at the great feast—are recited. We will alternate in reading the verses from Psalms 113 and 114.

*Men
& Boys:*   Alleluia!
You servants of Yahweh, praise,
Praise the name of Yahweh!
Blessed be the name of Yahweh,
Henceforth and forever!
From east to west,
Praised be the name of Yahweh!

*Women
& Girls:*   High over all nations,
Yahweh's glory transcends the heavens!
Who is like Yahweh our God?
Enthroned so high, Yahweh needs to stoop
To see the sky and earth!

Men
& Boys: Yahweh raises the poor from the dust;
          Lifts up the needy from the dunghill
          To give them a place with princes,
          With the princes of Yahweh's people.
          Yahweh enthrones the barren women in her
          house by making her the happy mother of sons
          and daughters.

Women
& Girls: Alleluia!
          When Israel came out of Egypt,
          the House of Jacob from a foreign nation,
          And Israel from Egypt's domain.

Men
& Boys: The sea fled at the sight,
          The Jordan stopped flowing,
          The mountains skipped like rams,
          And the hills like lambs.

Women
& Girls: Sea, what makes you run away?
          Jordan, why stop flowing?
          Why skip like rams, you mountains,
          Why like lambs, you hills?

Men
& Boys: Quake, earth, at the coming of your God,
          At the coming of the God of Jacob,
          Who turns rocks into pools,
          Flint into fountains.

III. Traditional Passover Prayers

Leader: The first act of the Jewish Passover is a benedic-
          tion, the *Kiddush*. The parent takes a cup of wine
          and recites this blessing:

Parent: Blessed are you, O Lord our God, Ruler of the uni-

verse, Creator of the fruit of the vine. Blessed are you, O Lord our God, Ruler of the universe, who has chosen us among all peoples and sanctified us with your commandments. In love you have given us, O Lord our God, solemn days of joy and festive seasons of gladness, even this day of the feast of the unleavened bread, a holy convocation, a memorial of the departure from Egypt. You have chosen us for your service and have made us sharers in the blessing of your holy festivals. Blessed are you, O Lord our God, who has preserved us, sustained us, and brought us to this season.
(*All take up their cups.*)

Leader: We who are Christians know, as Luke writes (22:18) that on the night Jesus celebrated the Pasch with his disciples, he said:
From now on, I tell you, I shall not drink wine until the kingdom of God comes."
(*All drink of the wine.*)

Leader: The next traditional act of the Jewish Passover meal is eating the greens. The greens are a symbol that nature comes to life in springtime. Following Jewish custom, we dip the greens in salt water and pray:

Parent: Blessed are you, O Lord our God, Ruler of the universe, Creator of the fruit of the earth.
(*All eat of the greens dipped in salt water.*)

Leader: Another action of the Jewish Passover meal is breaking the matzo. The Father lifts up the matzo and says:

Parent: Lo, this is the bread of affliction which our fathers and mothers ate in the land of Egypt. Let all who are hungry come and eat. Let all who are in

want come and celebrate the Passover with us. May it be God's will to redeem us from all trouble and from all servitude. Next year at this session may the whole house of Israel be free.
(The parent replaces the matzo on its plate.)

IV. The Questions

Leader: At the ancient Passover meal, the youngest child asked the parent four traditional questions about the Passover. In time, in order to carry on the discussion about the symbolic foods, other questions were also asked about their meanings. In more recent times, the same four questions have been asked at the *Seder*. The questions we ask tonight are similar but have been adapted to bring to mind the relationships between the Hebrew and Christian Scriptures.

Child: Why is this night different from all other nights?

Parent: In the *Mishnah* we find the ancient teaching of the Jews concerning the meaning of the Passover meal:

In every generation a person must so regard self as if he or she came forth out of Egypt, for it is written: "And you shall tell your children in that day saying, 'It is because of that which the Lord did for me when I came forth out of Egypt'" (Exodus 13:8). Therefore are we bound to give thanks, to praise...and to bless Yahweh who wrought all these wonders for our fathers and mothers and for us. Yahweh brought us out from bondage to freedom, from sorrow to gladness, and from mourning to a festival day, and from darkness to great light, and from servitude to redemption: so let us lay before Yahweh the *Hallel*, our song of praise.

We who are followers of Jesus know that as God rescued the Israelites through Moses from the slavery of Egypt, so God called us through Christ to leave our slavery to sin. Christ passed from this world to his Father, showing us the way and preparing a place for us, as he said: "No one can come to God except through me" (John 14:6).

Paul tells us in his letter to the church at Corinth: "And for anyone who is in Christ, there is a new creation; the old creation has gone, and now the new one is here" (II Corinthians 5:17). And again he wrote: "Now, however, you have been set free from sin, you have been made slaves of God, and you get a reward leading to your sanctification and ending in eternal life. For the wage paid by sin is death; the gift given by God is eternal life in Christ Jesus our Lord" (Romans 6:22-23).

Child: Why do we eat bitter herbs tonight at the special meal?

Parent: The Jews of old ate bitter herbs on Passover night, as do the Jews today, because "our ancestors were slaves in Egypt and their lives were made bitter." We who are followers of Jesus the Christ do not hesitate to taste of this bitterness as a reminder of his passion and death and to recall that he said: "Anyone who does not carry his or her cross and come after me cannot be my disciple" (Luke 14:27).
(All eat a bitter herb.)

Child: Why do we eat herbs tonight, and this time with sweet jam?

Parent: We dip the bitter herbs into the *haroses*, sweet jam, as did the Jews of old, as a sign of hope. Our ancestors were able to withstand the bitterness of slavery because it was sweetened by the hope of freedom. We who are followers of Christ are reminded that by sharing in the bitterness of Christ's sufferings we strengthen our hope. Paul writes in his letter to the church in Rome (5:2-5):

It is by faith and through Jesus that we have entered this state of grace in which we can boast about looking forward to God's glory. But that is not all we can boast about; we can boast about our sufferings. These sufferings bring patience, as we know; and patience brings perseverance, and perseverance brings hope, and this hope is not deceptive, because the love of God has been poured into our hearts by the Holy Spirit which has been given us.

Christ and his disciples—and all Jews who celebrate the Passover—tell the *Haggadah* during the Paschal meal. *Haggadah* means "retelling." It is the retelling of the Israelites' salvation from the tenth plague because the lintels of their doors had been marked with the blood of the lamb sacrificed at God's command and of the story of the exodus of the Jews from Egypt.

The yearly retelling of the deliverance of the Jews is an essential act in the Passover meal. As the evidence of God's loving care is refreshed in the minds of each individual each year, so is the renewal of their dependency upon God for all things, particularly their freedom from slavery.

(*All dip a second bitter herb in haroseth and eat it.*)

Child: Why did the Jews at the time of Jesus eat the Paschal Lamb when they celebrated the Passover meal?

Parent: At the time of the liberation from Egypt, at God's command each family took a lamb, sacrificed it, ate it, and sprinkled its blood on the doorpost and lintel. And on that night, seeing the blood, the angel of the Lord passed over them, killing the

Egyptians and sparing the Israelites. The Jews continued a memorial sacrifice of the lamb in the Temple for each family in Jerusalem at the time of the Passover. The lamb was brought home, roasted and eaten in a memorial meal. Since the destruction of the Temple in Jerusalem, there is no longer sacrifice but the meaning of the Paschal Lamb is retold by Jewish people today.

Followers of Jesus the Christ know that he is our Lamb, who sacrificed himself for us, and by his death and resurrection, enabled us to pass with him into eternal life with God. As Paul says: "Christ our Passover has been sacrificed" (I Corinthians 5:7).

(*All eat a piece of the lamb.*)

Child: Why did Christ and his disciples wash at table?

Parent: At the festival table of the Jews it is customary to wash the hands of all present while saying this prayer:

"Blessed are you, O Lord our God, Ruler of the universe, who sanctified us with your commandments and commanded us concerning the washing of hands."

On this night followers of Christ are taught a new meaning. Jesus, while washing the feet of his disciples, taught his commandment of love and service for others:

"The greatest among you must be servant. Anyone who exalts self will be humbled, and anyone who humbles self will be exalted." (Matthew 23:11)

Child: Why did Jesus and his disciples eat unleavened bread at the Passover meal?

Parent: The blessing and the breaking of the matzo is one of the important parts of the feast of the Pasch. The origin of the matzo was this:

"When Pharaoh let our ancestors go from Egypt, they were forced to flee in great haste. They had not time to bake their bread; they could not wait for the yeast to rise. So the sun beating down on the dough as they carried it along baked it into a flat, unleavened bread."

The matzo was the "bread of affliction" that enabled the Chosen people to be delivered from slavery.

On this night the followers of Christ recall that before Jesus distributed the bread to all his disciples, he added the significant words that we hear in the eucharistic celebration. Through this action all are able to become one in Christ, as Paul says: "The fact that there is only one loaf means that, though there are many of us, we form a single body because we all share in this one loaf" (I Corinthians 10:17).

(*The parent now takes a matzo and breaks off a portion, passes the matzo around and each eats a portion of it.*)

Child: Why did Jesus and his disciples drink wine at the Last Supper?

Leader: The feast of the Passover begins and ends with the drinking of a cup of wine. It is both a blessing and a thanksgiving expressed in this benediction prayer:

Parent: Blessed are you, O Lord our God, Ruler of the universe, creator of the fruit of the earth; you have given us this bread and wine to offer.
(*All present take a sip of wine.*)

Leader: On this night the followers of Jesus read in the gospel according to Luke:

All: "When the hour came he took his place at table, and the apostles with him. And he said to them,

'I have longed to eat this passover with you before I suffer; because, I tell you, I shall not eat it
again until it is fulfilled in the kingdom of God.'
Then taking the cup, he gave thanks and said,
'Take this and share it among you, because from
now on I tell you, I shall not drink wine until the
reign of God comes.' Then he took some bread,
and when he had given thanks, broke it and gave
it to them, saying, 'This is my body which will be
given for you; do this as a memorial of me.' He
did the same with the cup after supper, and said,
'This cup is the new covenant in my blood which
will be poured out for you'" (Luke 22:15-20).

Leader: For the Christian, then, this is the night of the
new Passover. Let us recall with respect the feast
of the Passover and its place in God's providence.
Let us recall with gratitude how on this night Jesus introduced a new memorial for his followers.
By this act and by his death and resurrection, he
established a new sacrifice, a new deliverance.

V. The Concluding Hallel

Leader: We shall all join in reciting the concluding psalm
(118) of the *Hallel,* keeping in mind that Matthew tells us:
"After psalms had been sung, they left for the Garden of Ol-
ives" (Matthew 26:30).

(Alternate verses between men and boys, and women and
girls.)

*Women
& Girls:*   Alleluia!
Give thanks to Yahweh for Yahweh is good,
Yahweh's love is everlasting!
Let the House of Israel say it,
Yahweh's love is everlasting!

*Men
& Boys:*   Let the House of Aaron say it,

Yahweh's love is everlasting!
Let those who fear Yahweh say it,
Yahweh's love is everlasting!

Women
& Girls: Hard pressed, I invoked Yahweh,
Yahweh heard me and came to my relief.
With Yahweh on my side, I fear nothing:
what can anyone do to me?

Men
& Boys: I would rather take refuge in Yahweh
than rely on people;
I would rather take refuge in Yahweh
than rely on princes.

Women
& Girls: I was pressed, pressed about to fall,
but Yahweh came to my help;
Yahweh is my strength and my song,
Yahweh has been my savior.

Men
& Boys: No, I shall not die, I shall live
to recite the deeds of Yahweh.
Though Yahweh has tried me often,
Yahweh has not abandoned me to death.

Women
& Girls: Open the gates of virtue to me,
I will come in and give thanks to Yahweh.
This is Yahweh's gateway
through which the virtuous may enter.

Men
& Boys: You are my God, I give you thanks,
I extol you, my God;
I give you thanks for having heard me,
you have been my savior.

All: Give thanks to Yahweh, for Yahweh is good, Yahweh's love is everlasting!

Leader: We have heard God's Word; we have shared a Paschal meal of the Old Covenant and the New Covenant, and we share the great gift of Jesus to us: his body and blood in bread and wine, in each other. For where two or three are gathered in Jesus' name, he is also present. Now let us go in the peace and love of Jesus, who is the Christ.

All: Thanks Be To God!

VI. Final Song

(All sing: melody: "When the Saints Go Marching In." Words are pronounced phonetically.) (Loose translation: When peace will come, we can return to the Promised Land.)

> Vukshay yavo, yavo shalom
> Vukshay yavo, yavo shalom
> As barakivet neesa I'demesek
> Vukashay yavo, yavo shalem!

Easter to Pentecost

Easter Symbols, Customs, and Rituals

Easter is the church's greatest feast. The mystery we celebrate at this time is at the very heart of our faith: Jesus, after his death on the cross, has risen from the tomb and we will, too, because he did. Joy and victory are the key themes of the Easter Vigil and Easter Sunday liturgies. The only adequate expression for these days is the often repeated: *Alleluia!*

Easter People

The sun has a natural significance which connects it with the resurrection theme. Early peoples attributed to the sun a great power because it dispelled darkness and brought the new day. This is also true of Christ, who dispelled the darkness of evil and sin to bring a new day of truth and life.

The gospel writers place the resurrection of Jesus near dawn on the first day of the week—*Sun*day—linking the natural symbol with the central belief of Christianity.

Because of this, the earliest Christians met on the first day of each week for the breaking of Bread and commemorating the life, death, and resurrection of Jesus. They saw themselves as people of the sun. Today the tradition of *Sun*day as a day of rest and worship in memory of Christ's resurrection continues to make us a people of the sun—an Easter people.

Easter Lilies

The Easter lily is larger than the more generally known Madonna lily. It was introduced in Bermuda from Japan at the middle of the last century. In 1882 the florist W.K. Harris brought it to the United States and spread its use here. Since it flowers first around Easter time in this part of the world, it soon came to be called the Easter lily. The American public immediately accepted the implied suggestion and make it a symbolic feature of the Easter decoration on Easter day, and people adopted it as a favorite in their homes for the Easter solemnities.

Although the Easter lily did not directly originate from a religious symbolism, it has acquired that symbolism, and quite appropriately so. Its radiant whiteness, the delicate beauty of shape and its bugle form, make it an eloquent herald of the Easter celebration. Lilies have always been symbols of beauty, perfection and goodness, and so appear in the holy Scriptures, both the Hebrew and the Christian Scriptures, bearing this symbolism.

Jesus once showed his disciples some lilies and said, "Not even Solomon in all his glory was arrayed like one of these" (Matthew 6:28). Now, since Jesus himself states that lilies are more glorious than the greatest earthly splendor, it is fitting that we use these beautiful flowers to commemorate his glory on the day of his resurrection.

Easter Eggs

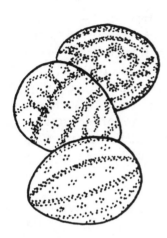

In ancient times Easter eggs were a symbol of spring and fertility. An egg seems dead and yet contains new life; so does the earth at the end of winter. This is the reason why people in pre-Christian ages presented each other with eggs at the beginning of spring, which in those days also was the beginning of the new year.

In medieval times the eating of eggs was prohibited during Lent. So the faithful transferred the custom of giving eggs to Easter Sunday. Instead of representing fertility, the Easter egg now became a symbol of the rock tomb out of which Christ gloriously emerged to the new life of his resurrection. The church even has a ritual blessing for eggs.

Blessing the Easter Eggs

The whole household can gather to bless the eggs that have been decorated for Easter. All extend their hands over the eggs as one member of the household prays the blessing:

> We praise you, O God, for these signs of life, our Easter eggs. We thank you for the bright, bursting forth of Christ our Lord. Amen. Alleluia!

In the same way, the household can bless the Easter pastries:

> We praise you, O God, for sweetness and delight. We thank you for the journey of Lent. We rejoice in the resurrection of Christ and this Eastertime. Amen. Alleluia!

Easter Water

In the liturgy of Holy Saturday night, the presider solemnly blesses the Easter water, which will be used during the service for baptisms. Families can take home a small container of this holy water to be used during the Easter season and the year for family blessings on persons, house, and rooms, and on Easter symbols such as eggs, pastry, baskets, meals. Each sprinkling signifies that all of our life is being baptized or being made holy by the presence of Christ to us.

During the year, parents can sign their children with a blessing using the holy water before tucking them into bed.

Family Paschal Candle

Burn a large white candle in your home at Eastertime, just as the Easter candle lights the sanctuary at church during Eastertime. Decorate it with the traditional symbols that are on the Paschal Candle, or any Christian or springtime symbols the family would like to have on their candle (nail polish or acrylic paints work best for this).

The Paschal Candle is inscribed with an *alpha* (the first letter of the Greek alphabet) and an *omega* (the last letter) with a cross in between. The four quarters of the cross are identified with the numerals of the current year.

Put your candle in a prominent place and you will have your very own Paschal Candle to remind you that Christ is our light.

Blessing for the Candle: After the candle is decorated and put in place, the head of the household can pray a blessing on the candle while all family members extend their hands over the candle:

> Loving God, we ask your blessing on this symbol of Christ our Light. May it be a constant reminder to all of us that we, too, are to bring the Light of Christ to others by our lives of justice and kindness. Amen.

In Greece it is a custom after the Easter Vigil to carry the "light" from the Paschal Candle home to light the lamps in each home. All our light comes from the one light—Christ. Your family may wish to carry a light from the Paschal Candle home to light your family Paschal Candle for the first time. (A glass enclosed votive candle works well for this "transport.")

Easter Bunny

Hares and rabbits served our pre-Christian ancestors as symbols of fertility because they multiply so fast. They were kept in homes and given as presents at the beginning of spring. From this ancient custom developed the story of the "Easter bunny" in Germany, in the 15th century. Little children believe that Easter eggs are produced and brought by the Easter bunny. It has no deep meaning, nor any religious background. In fact, the Easter bunny has never assumed religious symbolism like the Easter egg. Neither in liturgy nor in folklore do we find these animals connected with the spiritual significance of the Easter season, and there is no special blessing for rabbits or hares in the Roman Ritual.

Easter Lamb Cake

The Easter Lamb, representing Christ, with the flag of victory, is one of the most significant symbols of the festive season. It may be seen in pictures and images in the homes of most families in Catholic parts of Europe. The liturgical use of the Paschal Lamb as a symbol for the risen Christ inspired the faithful of medieval times to eat lamb on Easter Sunday.

For further explanation of the tradition behind the symbol, refer to the earlier described Seder or Paschal Meal.

Easter Pastry

In many countries of Europe people serve traditional breads and pastries at Easter like the Russian Easter bread (*Paska*), the German Easter loaves (*Osterstollen*), the Polish Easter cake (*Baba Wielanocna*), etc. Very often these breads and pastries, together with meat and eggs, are blessed on Holy Saturday. An Italian custom is to make a simple sweet bread dough shaped in the form of a chick, bunny, or doll. These breads are baked with a whole egg placed in the "tummy" of the form and frosted with egg yolk. The whole family is involved in the making of these Easter breads. They are brought to the Easter Vigil to be blessed and are given as gifts on Easter Sunday to young friends and relatives.

The Easter Food Basket

The blessing of the food, *Swiecone*, is a Polish custom performed on Holy Saturday. (All food which a Polish family eats on Easter Day is blessed on Holy Saturday.) This breakfast is called *Swiecone*. The egg, the symbol of life, is broken and shared with an exchange of good wishes. The Polish people have no special menu for Easter Day. There are no courses. Food aplenty is arranged upon sprigs of green leaves. Unlike Christmas, which is a day of family gathering, Easter in Poland is an occasion of traditional Polish hospitality when everybody is invited and welcomed. Perhaps this is the origin of our Easter basket.

Easter Clothes

The tradition of wearing new clothes on Easter Sunday is practiced by many people in this country, even by those who otherwise pay little attention to the spiritual side of the feast. This custom goes back to the early centuries of Christianity.

The early Christians, most of whom were adults when they were baptized during the solemn Easter vigil on the night of Holy Saturday, used to wear white gowns throughout the whole Easter week as a symbol of their new life. The other Christians, who had already been baptized in previous years, did not wear white garments, but they dressed in new clothes at Easter to indicate that they, too, had risen to a new life in Christ, had put off the old way and put on Jesus' way. Thus the wearing of new clothes at Easter was an external profession and symbol of the Easter grace, of a spiritual resurrection to a better and holier life.

Emmaus Day: Monday After Easter

Luke's gospel (24:13-35) tells the story of the two disciples on their way from Jerusalem to Emmaus and how they meet a stranger. The stranger asks them why they are so sad, and they tell him about the execution of Jesus. So the three walk on together and the stranger explains to them about Jesus and why he had to die in order to rise. Finally, they dine together at Emmaus, and as they break bread the two disciples recognize that the stranger is Jesus: "It is the Lord!" In their sadness they had not been able to recognize him.

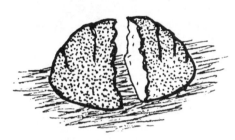

Celebrating Emmaus Day (Easter Monday) in your house might go like this: List four places that you've always said "Someday we must go there," but you have never gone, e.g., the zoo, the museum, a lake, a special restaurant, a park, an old friend's or a distant relative's.

Now make a family decision about your goal for this year's Emmaus Day outing. (If Easter Monday is not a good day, also decide on a date.) Talk about who will do what to be ready.

Before setting out, read together Luke 24:13-35. Then, with a little traveling music, set out. If possible, take a kind of transportation that will be special: walking, bicycling, taking the bus. Make the trip something of a storytelling time, warning everyone ahead of time to have a story to share.

On the way home, talk about how you met and recognized Christ on your journey.

Eastertime Daily Prayer

The arrival of Easter is not the time to discontinue the good beginnings experienced during Lent. Eastertime has its own way of praying together. Following are some suggestions:

Morning Prayer: Face east toward the rising sun. Raise arms to shoulder level, palms up. Then, with head up, raise arms slowly above head saying:

Glory to the Father
Glory to Jesus
Glory to the Spirit.

Slowly lower your arms and conclude with: "May God watch over us and bless us today."

Evening Prayer: Mom or Dad could begin by thanking God for the blessings of the day. Children will soon add to the prayer of thanks. Another night it might be a prayer for others, a prayer of forgiveness, a prayer of praise, etc. If this is done consistently, in time all of those prayer forms will become part of the family night prayer. This is also a good time to begin teaching the little ones some of our traditional memorized prayers.

Sit quietly for awhile and watch the setting sun. If you have the record, play the sunset theme from Ferde Grofés *Grand Canyon Suite*.

Mealtime Prayer: Mealtime is a good time to begin spontaneous prayer in your home. But spontaneous prayer can become as repetitious as memorized prayer with children. If this is the case, try making and using a family prayer wheel.

Cut a round circle out of heavy cardboard. Draw pie-shaped wedges on it. On each of the sections, print the family's suggestions for prayer. With a brad, attach an arrow in the center of the circle so that the arrow spins freely. Each day before the family meal, someone spins the arrow to select the prayer suggestion for that day. Anyone may add to the prayer in keeping with the chosen suggestion.

A Springtime Nature Walk

A springtime nature walk is a good family activity that will provide an opportunity for the family to witness the renewal of life on the natural level. Plan your nature walk for a mild day, allow plenty of time, and if possible, go to a nearby park or wooded area to which you can return later to observe additional seasonal changes.

Look for violets, ferns, and grasses sprouting from between dead leaves; note tree branches about to bloom; look and listen for toads, birds, and insects. Sniff!

Bring a box or bag so you can take home some small signs of new life. You can display these later as a table centerpiece or help the children make a simple dish garden or terrarium with mosses, grasses, and blossoming branches.

The Fortieth Day: Ascension Day

Read the first chapter of Acts. Spend some time looking at the clouds (sprawl on the ground for this). Clouds in our Scriptures and in the religion of many other peoples have a closeness to God because they are so like spirits. They are felt to be a hovering presence of the Lord.

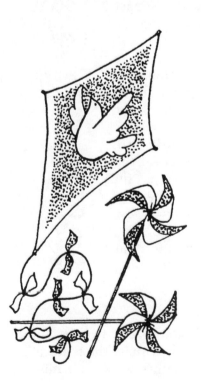

The Fiftieth Day: Pentecost

Read the second chapter of Acts. On Pentecost, those folks heard a wind, they breathed deeply, they felt the presence of God swirling about them and filling their very selves. They knew the Spirit when it happened to them!

So today we celebrate this wonderful way to know the closeness of God: the God manifest in the breezes and the wind storms of the earth, the God manifest in our own breathing. Celebrate! Blow, breathe, inhale, exhale, hold your breath, run out of breath, chase the wind, blow hard, inspire, expire, puff, gasp, wheeze, whistle, fly kites, blow soap bubbles, play wind instruments, make pin wheels, receive the Holy Spirit!

Summertime Rituals

Summer often becomes a time when family prayer and ritual discontinues. The following may provide opportunities to maintain a prayer/ritual process throught the year.

Prayer/Ritual Before a Vacation

When all is in readiness for the vacation, i.e. when all plans are finalized, bags are packed, and people are in readiness, gather all people and luggage together and pray:

> Blessed are you, God of Life and Leisure,
> You created a wide and wonderful world
> in which we can travel.
> We ask your blessing upon us as we prepare to leave
> on our journey of rest and relaxation.
> Be our companion on this journey.
> Make the road ahead of us free of harm and evil.
> Send your journeyers of old Abraham, Moses, Mary,
> Jesus with us.
> May we see all the beauty and wonder
> of your creation in our travels,
> and may we also see the beauty and wonder of each
> other in our trip.
> Bless us all as we set off.
> Bring us safely and peacefully home. Amen.

On return from vacation, remember to pray a prayer of thanks.

Ritual for the First Day of Summer (June 21)

A good time and place for this ritual is outdoors around sunset.

During the day, have the family collect symbols of summertime: wild and domestic flowers, weeds, grasses, summer fruits and vegetables, a container of earth, insects, a bowl of water (if you have goldfish, that can serve nicely). Gather all the symbols together around a lighted candle. Have a recording of the second movement ("Summer") of Vivaldi's *Four Seasons* playing softly in the background.

As the music is playing and the family becomes quiet, invite people to touch each of the symbols reverently. Then,

pray Francis of Assisi's "Canticle of All Creation." Take turns praying each of the verses while everyone else does the ritual gesture.

(*Arms and faces raised toward the sky.*) Most High, all powerful, all good God! All praise is yours, all glory, all honor, and all blessing. To you alone, Most High, does our praise belong.

(*Face the sun with arms extended.*) All praise be yours, my Lord, through all that you have made, and first to Brother Sun, who bring the day, and light you give us through him. How beautiful is he, how radiant in all his splendor! Of you, Most High, he bears the likeness.

(*Face the direction that the moon will rise, arms extended.*) All praise be yours, my Lord, through Sister Moon and Stars, in the heavens you have made them bright and precious and fair.

(*Face the direction from which the wind is blowing.*) All praise be yours, my Lord, through Brothers Wind and Air, both fair and storm, all the weather's moods, by which you cherish all that you have made.

(*Touch the water.*) All praise be yours, my Lord, through Sister Water, so useful, lowly, precious and pure.

(*Touch the candle.*) All praise be yours, my Lord, through Brother Fire, through whom you brighten up the night. How beautiful his is. Full of power and strength.

(*Touch the ground.*) All praise be yours, my Lord, through Sister Earth, our Mother. She feeds us in her power and produces fruits, colored flowers and herbs. (*Touch the fruits, flowers, and grasses.*)

(*Put arms around each other.*) All praise be yours, my Lord, through those who grant pardon for love of you; those who endure sickness and trial, happy those who live in peace, they will be crowned.

All: Praise and bless the Lord, and give thanks.

Have the family share personal prayers of thanks and praise for creation and for the gifts of summertime.

This ritual can be adapted to include a blessing of the family garden if you have one. After a blessing prayer for the seeds and seedlings that have been planted, have each family member water a part of the garden.

Blessing for the First Day of School

Although the church year begins with Advent, our culture tends to mark time by the school year. Rather than fight culture, perhaps we can Spiritualize the reality. A good way to do this is to have a special family ritual blessing for the first day of school. This ritual can begin the evening before.

Gather the family and all the newly purchased school supplies and new school clothes. Spend some time talking about hopes and fears the children may have about the new school year. The kindergartner may be frightened, the first grader may be anxious because she or he can't read and will be expected to.

Youngsters moving into junior or senior high school have their own special anxieties. Talk about them.

After the family sharing, have the whole family pray a blessing over the new school supplies.

Blessing of New School Supplies

Parent: God of Life and Newness
Be with us here today
as we look to and prepare for the new school year.
We ask you to bless these school supplies gathered here.
May they always be used for good
And may they help those who use them
learn more about you and your people.

(Each child then prays over the various supplies with hands extended in blessing.)

Child: Bless this paper, waiting to bear the knowledge and creativity of the writer.

Child: Bless these pens, pencils and crayons. May they write and color beauty, and truth.

Child: Bless these notebooks and portfolios. May they help to keep us organized.

Child: Bless these lunch boxes (bags, lunch tickets). May their contents nourish our bodies so that our minds will be bright and active.

Child: Bless these new school clothes. May they be a sign

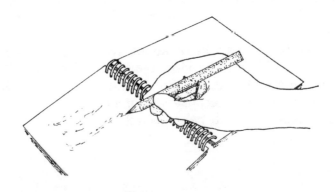

of the joy, hope, and new life that we bring to this new school year.

Parent: God of New Beginnings, bless these children and their schoolsupplies. Be with them during this new year of learning. May they experience new knowledge, new friends, new joy, new peace and new life. (*Sprinkle school supplies and children with holy water.*)

Blessing of Children on the First Day of School

On the morning of the first day of school, as the children are ready to leave, gather them together for a simple "sending forth" blessing:

Parent(s):   God of Love,
Bless these children whom I (we) love.
Watch over them as they go forth
into their world of school.
Open their minds to the knowledge
that will be given them,
and protect them in all their encounters.
(*Trace a sign of the cross on the forehead of each child.*)

Autumn Rituals

Apples

For a family harvest festival, take one whole day and go to an apple orchard where you can pick your own. Learn to tell one kind of apple from another (a Delicious from a Winesap or a Jonathan from a MacIntosh). Discover your favorites for eating. Bring back many kinds and have an all-apple meal: cider, dumplings for the main course, pie for dessert.

Before your apple meal, or just after you've picked a beautiful bushel, gather in a circle and all extend hands over the apples to bless them. "Blessed are you, O Lord our God, ruler of the universe, for giving us the fruit of the apple tree."

Then each person picks an apple. All together say the alphabet as each turns the stem. When the stem breaks, the alphabet is interrupted for a moment and that person praises God for something beginning with the letter the stem broke on. Continue reciting the alphabet until another person's apple-stem breaks off, and a prayer of praise is offered.

Save your appleseeds! Later that night, spread them out on the table and tell the story of John Chapman who got to be known as Johnny Appleseed—a real hero of the American frontier who had friends of all colors and carried only the Bible and his appleseeds.

At bedtime say this prayer: "Keep us, O Lord, as the apple of your eye!"

Leaves

On the day you rake your yard, make the biggest pile of leaves you've ever seen. High! Wide! Deep! Get as many people as possible to jump into the leaf pile. Take a few favorite leaves to the family dinner table, arrange them in the center and listen to a recording of "Autumn Leaves." Share hot cocoa and toasted marshmallows. Then each person holds up a leaf and pray a prayer of praise and thanks for autumn's beauty and the day's fun.

Halloween

The last day of October, commonly known as Halloween in our culture, actually has a religious origin and tradition. The tradition is that folks went from door to door on this day requesting food for the less fortunate. Often people dressed as saints who gave to those less fortunate.

For today's children, the celebration of Halloween has maintained the element of pretending that they are someone else. However, it has lost the element of soliciting for the less fortunate—except for those who travel with UNICEF boxes.

Agree as a family, that one-half of each child's Halloween booty be donated to a local food shelf along with some nutritious food, as well. It could be a great way to celebrate the next day, All Saints, by being today's "saints" marching into the lives of the poor with symbols of health and hope for others.

All Saints—November 1
This is *our* day, the day when we celebrate the household called church. How about a neighborhood or block progressive dinner: salad at one home, main course at another, dessert at another, and so on? As you progress from house to house, the whole group could sing "When the Saints Go Marching In."

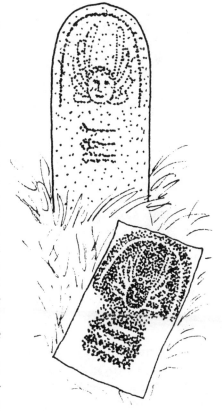

All Souls—November 2
Early in November we have a day for remembering all the dead. One way to do this would be to visit a cemetery. Take along some large pieces of paper and some crayons. Make rubbings on the grave stones, especially the very old ones. (Rubbings are made by placing a piece of paper on the stone, holding it still while rubbing all over it with a crayon. The paper then shows the words and designs of the stone.) Notice the poems on some of the stones, the loving words on others, the dates that show the age of the person.

Cemeteries are often beautiful places for a picnic. In some countries, people bring the favorite foods of a friend or relative who has died and have a picnic near the grave. It is a way of remembering how special each person was. At home, the rubbings can decorate the wall during November.

A Victory Book
Make a beautifully decorated list of those who have died whom you want to remember in prayer throughout the month—relatives, neighbors, friends, people who were famous, people whom no one else remembers. This, too, can be made large enough to become a wall decoration that will act as a reminder for the family.

November Menu Special

Doughnuts are a special November food: The circle reminds us of the circle of life and death: the seed springs to life, grows, matures, produces its fruit with new seeds, and dies. But now there is a new seed. The circle has no end. Make doughnuts as a family and enjoy eating them together.

Campaign for Human Development Dinner
The week of the Campaign for Human Development can become more personal for your family. Choose one day during the week when you have a meal comparable to the meals usually eaten by nearly two-thirds of the world's people. Have your family share a meal which costs no more than three dollars for the whole family, or share a meal of rice and bread. Then give the money saved on food that day to the Campaign for Human Development.

Family Ritual for Thanksgiving
Some time between now and Thanksgiving have the family gather together to decorate a small box with an autumn or Thanksgiving motif. Make a slot in the cover of the box and decorate it in such a way so that it can be opened easily.

After the box is decorated, give each person in the family as many small pieces of paper as there are family members. Have each person write the special gift that each family member contributes to the rest of the family. Fold the paper and write the name of that person on the outside of the folded paper (e.g., Mom—bakes great pies, Oscar—the peacemaker of the family). Teens and parents can help preschoolers write theirs. If others are sharing Thanksgiving with you, include their names and gifts as well.

Use the box as the focal point of your Thanksgiving centerpiece. Then, just before the food is served (while it is all keeping warm in the oven), gather the family around the already set table, open the box and allow time for each person to read the papers with his or her name on them. Have someone in the family lead a prayer of thanks for the family, for the gifts present in the family, and then invite others to add whatever else for which they are thankful.

When the prayer is over, go to the kitchen as a family, where each person is given something to carry to the table for dinner.

Christ, the King

This feast, which follows the Sundays of Pentecost, deserves a special dessert: a bundt cake decorated like a crown in honor of Christ the King. (The cake can be decorated with colored gumdrops for jewels in the crown, the cake itself is crown-shaped.) Let the children help with the decoration of the cake.

Before eating the cake, pray Psalm 97 together: "The Lord is King! Let the earth rejoice and everyone be glad!"

Miscellaneous Blessings

To bless someone or something is to claim that person or thing for God. Simple blessings are a good way for the family to express their belief in our God who is ever protective of us. Following are some blessing rituals that may be useful at various times.

Blessing for a New Baby

On the day that the new baby comes home, the rest of the family gathers at the front door waiting to welcome the new family member. Those waiting can have a bouquet of flowers, a new piece of clothing for the baby, a new toy, and other things that the baby will be needing and using.

As the baby enters the home, together say "Welcome Home, N." (baby's name). Then form a procession to the nursery, led by the person with the flowers. In the nursery, all gather around the baby and one by one, each person trace the sign of the cross on the baby's forehead. While signing the baby, each person prays a special prayer of blessing for the baby. (For example, "_____ , may God bless you and protect you all the days of your life. We claim you for God and welcome you to our family.")

Blessing for a New Home

Materials needed:

A candle

A bowl of water

A pine or cedar branch for sprinkling water

Gather the family together in the family room. On a small table have the candle, bowl of water and branch. Light the candle and stand for a moment in silence. Then hold hands forming a circle around the table and sing, "Be it ever so humble there's no place like home." Then one of the children picks up the candle, one carrys the bowl of water and one carries the branch.

Parent: Bless our home and make it a home in which you would be comfortable, oh God. Send your

Holy Spirit into every nook and cranny. Let the walls respond with love and laughter. Let your birds sing in the trees outside and your flowers bloom in the garden.

Bless our family room and fill it with loving communication.
(*Each family member takes a turn dipping the branch into the bowl of water and sprinkles the room as each repeats the blessing prayer for the family room. This is repeated as the family processes to each room of the house, the child with the candle leading the procession to kitchen dining room, bedrooms, etc.*)

(*In the kitchen*)
Bless our kitchen and fill it with the warmth of shared bread.
(*All sprinkle the room, repeating the prayer.*)

(*In the dining room*)
Bless our dining room and the food and conversation we share here.
(*All sprinkle the room, repeating the prayer.*)

(*In each bedroom*)
Bless this bedroom. May (*name the person whose bedroom is being blessed*) be filled with restful sleep here.
(*All sprinkle the room, repeating the prayer.*)

(*In the bathroom*)
Bless this bathroom. May the spirit of health and healing abide here.
(*All sprinkle the room, repeating the prayer.*)

(*Outside the house*)
Bless the exterior of our home. Protect it from wind, rain, snow, and sun.

> (*All walk around the outside of the house sprinkling while repeating the prayer.*)
> (*At the front door*)
> Bless this doorway. May all who come to it be treated with kindness and hospitality.
> (*All sprinkle the doorway repeating the prayer.*)

(*Back in the family room*)
Parent: Bless each room and each of us, Dear God. Make yourself at home with us.
            (*All sign themselves with water.*)

Blessing for a New Car

Have each family member place a hand on the new car while one family member prays:

> God our Protector,
> we ask your blessing
> on this our new car.
> Bless it with your protection
> and protect, as well,
> all who ride in it.
> Watch over in a special way
> those who will drive this car
> that they will drive safely
> and always respect the rights of others.
> May the blessing of the Trinity,
> The Creator, the Redeemer and the Spirit
> (*all trace the sign of the cross on the car*)
> rest on this car and remain forever.
> Amen.

When the blessing prayer is completed, all help wash and wax the car. This can be like a huge sprinkling and anointing with oil.

Blessing for Someone Sick

God of health and wholeness,
your friend_____is sick

and desires to be well again.
Hear our prayer for the healing of
_____ whom we love so much.
Remove this illness from him/her.
Remove all that causes pain and sickness
so that he/she will be able to return
to a life of wholeness and health.
With faith and hope,
we call on the healing medicine of your grace.
We ask for healing, God,
and also for acceptance of your plan for
and for each of us.
(*Lay hands on the sick person.*)
_____, may you be blessed
with the power and love of God
and the care and affection
of those who love you. Amen.

Blessing for a Young Person Leaving Home

(*This blessing is especially appropriate for a young person leaving home for college.*)

Begin by reading Genesis 12: 1-4 Abram's journey to a new land. (*Parent(s) light a candle and begin to reflect on the the young person's birth and life. Other family members add fond remembrances of life with the person who is preparing to leave home.*)

Presention of Gifts:

We bring you soap, so that you may never be afraid to get your hands dirty in the service of your neighbor.
We bring you lotion, so that those hands may be soft for touching with love.
We bring you powder for your feet that they might carry you far, but never so far that they will not bring you home again.
We bring you a flower, that you might always bring joy to those you meet.Other gifts may also be presented.
The young person responds: I leave the home of childhood with joy, open to the new. And I will never forget all of you and the life and love you have given me.

All pray while placing a hand on the young person:
    As you have been loved, may you love.
    As you have been nurtured, may you nurture others.
    As you have been joy to us, may you be joy to others.
    May God go with you as you journey away from us,
    and may your journey always bring you full circle
    back to us often.

Notes for Your Family Rituals

Notes for Your Family Rituals

Notes for Your Family Rituals

Notes for Your Family Rituals